Searching for Sulis

Alan Richardson

Margaret Haffenden

Alan Richardson has been writing weird, winsome and frequently embarrassing books for longer than many of his readers have been alive and is insanely proud of that fact. He has done biographies of such luminaries as Dion Fortune, Aleister Crowley, Christine Hartley, William G. Gray and his own grandfather George M. Richardson M.M. & Bar. Plus novels and novellas that are all set in his local area, along with scripts of same. He has a deep interest in Earth Mysteries, Mythology, Paganism, Celtic lore, Ancient Egypt, jet fighters, army tanks, Wiltshire tea shops, Great British Actors and Newcastle United Football Club. He does not belong to any group or society and does not take pupils because most of the time he hasn't a clue what is going on.

Searching for Sulis is another totally indulgent book self-published via KDP

I don't have a web site, am not on LinkedIn, and I don't do blogs. A more detailed list of my published work can be found somewhere on Amazon Books.

Anyone with a pressing need to contact me can do so via: *alric@blueyonder.co.uk* but please don't attach your manuscripts and ask for 'an honest opinion' because I will always lie.

Dedicated to...

Dolores Ashcroft who taught me more than *anyone* about Magick

Karan Kanhai, who triggered this book off.

R.J. Stewart, whose seminal book *Waters of the Gap* should be compulsory reading for anyone trying to track down Sulis

Paul Dunne, who does so much Work behind the scenes without thought of reward.

Carolyn Moody for being a partner in Crone

Judith Page for opening many secret doors over many years

The occupants of NW3 4RG for always keeping their lights on

The late Rendel Harris and E.F. Wills for
their deliciously insane but inspirational pamphlet that I've included
in this book as a tribute to the Work they did in the 1930s.

Some published books

Geordie's War.
Aleister Crowley and Dion Fortune
The Inner Guide to Egypt *with Billie John*
Priestess - the Life and Magic of Dion Fortune
Magical Gateways
The Magical Kabbalah
The Google Tantra - How I became the first Geordie to raise the Kundalini.
new edition retitled as…
Sex and Light – how to Google your way to God Hood.
The Old Sod *with Marcus Claridge*
Working with Inner Light *with Jo Clark*
Spirits of the Stones.
Earth God Rising - the Return of the Male Mysteries.
Earth God Risen
Gate of Moon
Dancers to the Gods
Inner Celtia *with David Annwn*
Letters of Light
Me, mySelf and Dion Fortune
Bad Love Days
Short Circuits
The Templar Door

Fiction

The Giftie
On Winsley Hill
The Fat Git – the Story of a Merlin
The Great Witch Mum – *illustrated by Caroline Jarosz*
Dark Light – a neo-Templar Time Storm
The Movie Star
Shimmying Hips
du Lac
The Lightbearer
Twisted Light
The Moonchild

Sulis is the most important Goddess of current times as she contains the essence and lessons relevant to our present times and planetary predicament as a species.

Paul Dunne

This is a book about a little known Goddess called Sulis, whose time has now come, and who influences you whether you realise it or not. It is a loose journal about our local expeditions to visit sacred wells, ponds, rivers and streams within our area, while trying to find out more about Her and – if this doesn't sound too mawkish – about ourselves.

We will tell you about: obscure and near-forgotten deities that lurk behind us today, hidden wellsprings (on more than one level), dubious inner-plane beings, potent nursery rhymes, ancient hauntings, angry trolls, faery glades, phantom monks, enchanted tea-shoppes, Weeping Sisters, curses and healings, reincarnations of Dion Fortune and her family – and those simple Earth and Water Magicks you can all try at home that yet lead to the Stars.

And hopefully we will make each reader feel that they have been personally involved in our search.

Margaret Haffenden & Alan Richardson
Beltaine 2019

Is this…

Bel, Sul, Sulis, Bladud, Horus, Abaris, Fontus, Pontus
or
your own Higher Self?

Table of Contents

Chapter 1

But water always goes where it wants to go, and nothing in the end can stand against it. Water is patient. Dripping water wears away a stone. Remember that, my child. Remember you are half water. If you can't go through an obstacle, go around it. Water does.

Margaret Atwood, *The Penelopiad*

February 7th 2019

A Preliminary Droplet...

This was meant to be a straightforward local-interest book about the holy wells and sacred springs that are scattered around us in West Wiltshire. I had the idea that we would get waters from each and add them to the very small frog pond that we have at the end of our long and narrow garden. This is situated just before the old outbuilding known as Dad's Shed and in a corner we call the Zone Where Time Stops. This is because we hang old watches on a large bush there. The frog, when he does appear, seems very happy. Unlike the psychic pressures that resulted in a previous book *The Templar Door*, there was no sense of troubled revenants demanding attention before we started this one.

We planned to start on a particular day at the Temple of Sulis, in the nearby city of Bath and then, in a manner of speaking, follow whatever tributaries of knowledge and insight might flow from there.

What I didn't expect was the sudden and irritating appearance of the Fisher King and the sense of his parched Wasteland behind him.

I lost my awe of the Fisher King and the Holy Grail a long time ago. If you want to know why, I've included an essay about this in Appendix 3, so you might want to read that now. It's quite possible that you will find my attitude unsettling. On the other hand, it might get you out of stagnant waters...

So I've never liked the Fisher King. If he'd been aware of my minnow-like existence I'm sure the feeling would be mutual. I didn't expect him to come floating into my mind in the pre-dawn light of a bleak February morning but he did and he wouldn't go. So there he was, somewhere in my head, sitting in his lonely room in his remote castle, nursing the mysterious Wound on his thigh (medieval code for genitals) and looking out toward his realm that was, eternally, a dry and dead Wasteland. I had expected someone quite splendid but he looked over-weight and rather down-at-heel, like someone who had been doing pantomime in the same costume for a few seasons too many.

If you don't know anything about him then you may want to look him up yourself before we go any further. You see, he lures solitary pilgrims who are in search of the Holy Grail, but I personally lost interest in that spiritual dead-end some decades ago. When they get to him, appalled by the Wasteland but delayed in their quest by his righteous misery, then depending on which myth-line they follow, they are expected to ask a Question – or NOT ask a Question – else their quest will falter. They rarely get it right and they are left with him sitting there tut-tutting at their failure.

Was this truly a psychic connection with an inner plane being of exalted pedigree? Or just some hypnogogic processes in that delicious state before waking? To be honest I don't know. My wife is used to those states of mine wherein I'm convinced I'm awake, and aware of her puttering around in the room, whereas she is certain that I'm largely asleep. It's not something I worry about, the crucial point being that it was intensely real to me.

There was an exchange of ideas that came through then that I can best simplify in words, although these won't capture it easily.

Fisher King	What do you seek?
Me	Nothing. I'm not interested in your un-holy Grail.
Fisher King	Why are you here?
Me	I'm passing through. Your time has been and gone. Humans can self-heal and so can you. Heal yourself and let your land blossom.

Fisher King	What must you ask?
Me	Nothing. Heal yourself and go – and No, I'm not going to replace you.

Some readers will be offended by this. But honestly, I don't care if the virtue-signalling Fisher King was, as some say, descended via some dubious blood-line from what he called the Christ. That inner land of his has been in decay for endless centuries. In this day and age, when our outer world is falling apart, it's a disgrace.

During this exchange, while having a very real rainstorm bashing against the window of our bedroom, I was aware of another being entering the scene. This one stood behind me and slightly to my right side. He was young, slim, vigorous and with iridescent, multi-hued clothing. There was an air about him of taking notes. I think he – or it – was amused by the interplay.

I turned to face this new presence and did the wordless equivalent of asking:

*Are you here to take his place? Are **you** the new Fisher King?*

No. I'm here to meet you.

Who are you?

I'm Bladud he said, and smiled before he disappeared.

I'll tell you about Bladud in due course and even give a simple technique that offers unusual gates that can open toward such contacts. But I should explain how this whole project called 'Searching for Sulis' came about.

As I said, my wife Margaret and I had long muttered about doing something involving the numerous Holy Wells scattered around Wiltshire and its western boundaries with Somerset. We initially planned to visit Cat's Well, in Bratton, which is a small but rambling village on the northern edge of the Salisbury Plain. There is nothing feline connected with this little well, as the name is a contraction of St Catherine's Well. We simply wanted to scoop up a little water into a jar, go to the nearest tea rooms and read the morning papers, then drive back home to add the water to the tiny pond in our garden.

But as Imbolc and St Bridget's day was coming up on February 1st and 2nd. I had the idea that we should recognise this by making a pilgrimage to a place where Bridget/Bride/Bridey had once been worshipped right strongly under another form and name, as Sulis - hence the Roman name for our nearby town of Bath, known to them as Aquae Sulis.

That's when the worm-hole appeared. Well, not so much a star-gatey worm-hole as found in the glamorous realms of Quantum science and Occult pretend-science, but a whirlpool. And believe me, every one of you reading this will have known this whirlpool in your own terms: when suddenly a whole mass of realisations, connections, images and serendipities swirl together in the most unexpected ways. Events, memories, peoples, places and things you've done in the past suddenly whoosh together and make unexpected sense. You will find yourself exclaiming: *So that's why I did that!* or usually: *That's why this happened to me!* and you feel yourself being spun around and sucked into something quite marvellous with the cry: *Where is this taking me?*

Of course, as I write this in my little garden office during a sudden and truly apocalyptic hail storm on another sunny day, I'm uncomfortably aware of the parallels between this and the question that pilgrims are supposed to ask of the Fisher King.

Even so, I still don't like him.

So I was in my own whirlpool in those few days before we took the train into nearby Bath where the Temple of Sulis still provides the very rationale for that small city's existence. Until then I had assumed I had been brought to this area from far-off Northumberland by the beings who lay behind Dion Fortune, as I've explained at length elsewhere.[i] But with all sorts of other strange connections now whirling around I began to wonder if, in fact, the entities which brought me and also her family here were actually tied up with the goddess Sulis and the primordial energies behind what R.J. Stewart described as the 'Waters of the Gap'.

More of him later, too.

It seems that the hot springs at Bath were first used by Neolithic people at least 10,000 years ago, and developed by the Celts from around 700 BCE, when Sulis was probably already being worshipped. When the Legions arrived they named the place *Aquae Sulis* and saw in it a microcosm of Rome itself because it was also surrounded by seven hills. From around 70 CE they began to build the complex we see today which, apart from the underground Temple itself, involved a variety of baths offering numerous treatments. A million litres from this sacred spring erupts to the surface every day at a temperature of about 48 degrees centigrade. Forty-three minerals have been identified within its water and a high iron content causes the characteristic orange staining on the stonework. I don't want to burble much more at this stage lest I sound like a tourist guide. Like everything else now, readers can  probably find out the everyday details on their phones.

Entrance into the Roman Baths and the temple complex cost an eye-watering £32.00 for the two of us but I tried to look at this from a magickal angle, telling myself that this represented the 32 paths on the Tree of Life and not to be a skinflint when there was hot magick afoot. *Man up and stop whimpering* I told myself as I paid the attendant and we were offered little devices to hang around our necks that would give us a guided tour in a hundred languages.

I didn't use the thing but more or less hurtled from the ground level downward, ignoring the various baths themselves, not remotely interested in the shades of the Romans who once used them and so found myself at the actual Source. I knew that, with a bus-load of Japanese tourists behind me I wouldn't have much time to try and commune with whatever brought me – and Margaret – to this realm.

And I mean 'realm' in both the mundane and mystical senses of the word. And I use the word 'Source' in the same way.

Take it from me that there is a very marked atmosphere about this once sacrosanct area: any notion you might construct about sybilline priestesses and the original Goddess are likely to be more right than wrong.

'When in doubt, do nowt' should be chiselled on the porticos of such places, which I think would be more relevant to me than the *Gnothi Seauton* – or Man Know Thyself - that was on the forecourt of the Temple of Apollo at Delphi. I just stood there in the warm, moist alchemies of this outpouring from the ancient of days and watched the waters tumbling out of the dark hole, over the rocks and under my feet. There was a space to the right, with two steps leading directly to the cave, if I can call it that, but access was denied to the public.

Margaret joined me and we stood side by side, in silence. I saw the water as Light, emerging from the Source, pouring toward and through me. She did her own quiet and secret thing, working at a level far beyond me – though she would always deny that. Before we left, before the tourists arrived, we both spat into the waters and thus offered a part of ourselves to them.

But listen, if you were expecting cosmic revelations and Goddesses descending, then I must disappoint you. In fact I'd advise you to distrust any self-styled mage spouting such things. Although we both felt that we had been touched by the atmosphere of the place, and rather hoped that things might work themselves to the surface later, our main and outer concern was to get back upstairs to the glorious Pump Room, the Regency ballroom where they serve morning tea to the musick of a string trio.

I'm not being crass. It was either Dion Fortune – or it might have been Gareth Knight – who wrote somewhere that after a magickal working you should try to ground yourself by having a meal. For me this meant tea and hot crumpet smoored with local honey, and for

Margaret it was chocolate cake with strong coffee that made her eyes roll in her head.

It is on such occasions, in similar places that I have my own epiphanies, which are every bit as important as any of the things that happen on inner levels. Here, beneath the crystal chandeliers, within the soaring lemon-yellow walls and the floor-to-ceiling windows that looked out over the Abbey Courtyard, we mused upon the high strangeness of our separate lives that had brought us together in the oddest of ways.[ii] There are some lines by D.H. Lawrence, in the last paragraphs of *Apocalypse,* which was the last thing he ever wrote, that I've quoted many times elsewhere because of their huge impact on me over the years.

> For man, as for flower and beast and bird, the supreme triumph is to be most vividly, most perfectly alive. Whatever the unborn and the dead may know, they cannot know the beauty, the marvel of being alive in the flesh. The dead may look after the afterwards. But the magnificent here and now of life in the flesh is ours, and ours alone, and ours only for a time. We ought to dance with rapture that we should be alive and in the flesh, and part of the living, incarnate cosmos.

So here am I inwardly dancing with rapture with my gentle, beautiful, kind, witty, daft, brilliant and extraordinary wife, who is a cross between Beryl the Peril and Minerva, as we muse upon those private First Swirlings that brought us to this place and point in time.

I had an idea about the whirlpool again and tried to show off to her by creating one in my teacup with the spoon - both to make sense of it all and perhaps to honour the Goddess Sulis. I only succeeded in making a mess on the table cloth.

Bear with me again and I'll soon tell you more about Sulis/Bridget/Minerva, the Waters of the Gap or Eye, the Whirlpool, the god Bel and the flying Bladud, plus all the other wells and springs we planned to visit while exploring the consciousness of Water itself.

And most of all how I'll try and show how this is all relevant to yourselves, no matter where you live in the world.

I said earlier that I'd give you a simple technique you can use straight away. This was given by Tom Kenyon, who is one of the few channellers whose output I trust. I'd been using this on the night before the Fisher King appeared and began doing so the following morning when the exchange happened. I like it because it is simple. You don't have to robe up and do ponderous invoking rituals in your spare room, or yet prance naked, dancing widdershins in some woodland glade. (Neither of which, I would add, have ever been part of my own Work and neither of which I would mock in others.) He mentions briefly two Dragon Points within us where the heavenly *chi* flows into the body and meets the terrestrial (or earth) *chi* of the body itself. I confess I know nothing about *chi* but, as I say, I trust Kenyon's experience and teachings. He advises us to lie down, if we want, and just notice our breathing, without trying to change it in any way. Then:

> Then after a moment become aware of the space about an inch behind the bridge of the nose. imagine that there is an opening about one inch square in this area. This is the Celestial Gate. All you do is focus on it. Do not concentrate on it. Just be aware of it. If you are having thoughts or fantasies, this is not a problem. ... You can think all you want about anything you want and the practice will still work, so long as some part of your attention is on the Celestial Gate... As you explore your own inner worlds, you might eventually encounter celestial beings who may grace you with their guidance and instruction.[iii]

I suppose those 'celestial beings' he mentions may well have been those two figures of the aged Fisher King and young Bladud who floated into my awareness that morning. I had been creating the Celestial Gate awareness as he advised, but the image of the Source within the Roman Baths kept superimposing itself. Perhaps Bladud, who is intimately connected to this site as I shall explain, saw an opportunity to appear. At the time of writing this sentence, February 12th, I haven't seen him since.

But you can try this yourself. Place that image of the steaming waters pouring from the depths of the Earth into your mind and see what happens – if anything. This sort of 'remote viewing' or 'remote contacting' is pretty standard practice among many on the magickal path. I know of groups who use the image of caverns within Glastonbury Tor, meeting there in their imaginations at agreed times. I know of individuals who have used the trilithons of Stonehenge as imaginal gates; others who have used images of sacred lakes whose depths they have sought to explore on inner levels by, metaphorically and magickally, plunging in. Yet others, myself included, have constructed Egyptian temples in which to try and make contact with varying types of energies.

The crucial thing is, you must **work** at it. It is not so much *what* you do, but that you devise an entry-point into the Otherworld and then make enough determined effort that harmonious inner plane beings make their way toward you. Be original. Do your own thing. This the beginning of the true Work that you read about.

This might all sound a bit fuzzy at the moment, so we must look a little more closely at the actual names of the Beings connected with this outwardly expensive but inwardly priceless Temple of Sulis. After all, you can hardly go around shouting inside your mind: Hey You!

No-one knows with any certainty the absolute origins of the name 'Sulis'. R.J. Stewart, who wrote his seminal book *The Waters of the Gap* while living almost atop the Roman Baths, notes that in both Welsh and old Irish the word 'suil' or 'sulis' means an eye, gap or orifice. The natives of this area, in the West of what we now call England, would have used a native word such as this to create a natural name for the presiding goddess. As he wrote:

Divine names are almost always functional descriptions, not only of the god or goddess, but of the place of origin. It is sometimes difficult to separate the function and site of a divine being, as the worship was environmental and each sacred site was thought to be the magical 'centre of the world'.

The waters of Sul or Sulis, goddess of the gap, would have been particularly important to the Celts for two reasons. The first was that they considered water sources to be extremely sacred, and the second was that they had a religious concept of the creation of life within a boiling cauldron.[iv]

Her name may be related to the proto-Celtic word for Sun, from which the Old Irish súil (eye) was derived. Which probably leads to one of her titles as 'The Bright One'. There is also the Gaelic 'soilleir' which can mean, depending on context: transparent in colour; free of ambiguity; without clouds; bright, not obscured. And if I can risk taking the sound of the name to a greater extreme, then among Persians 'suhail' was a synonym of wisdom, illumination and brilliance. She also appears in multiple form as the tripartite *Suliviae*. The latter name is also used of the pan-Celtic divinity Brigid, suggesting a connection between these figures. The Celts, who honoured the sun on Beltane instead of the summer solstice, held their fire-festival on May 1 in reverence of Sulis.

This all gets very dense and intense but thank goodness these days I can invoke the all-knowing Thoth to get more insights. In this case (strictly between us!), I refer not to the ibis-headed Egyptian deity but to my beloved Google, which helps me to sound smarter than I actually am. So, using Google Trismegistus, accessing a site devoted to the Scottish Gaelic language, *Sùil* can mean 'Eye', or in another context 'Hope' – which they helpfully define as a belief that something wished for can happen. I'm not being snide when I quote this last because, as you will see, that was an intrinsic part of the peoples' belief in what Sulis could do for them. Later, we'll look at the 'curse tablets' that the Romano-Celts dropped into the sacred waters of the temple in a desperate need to ask for Sulis-Minerva's help in redressing wrongs.

But allow me a small yet important digression here...

For all its faults I see Google as a manifestation of the askashic records, with each web-entry seen through the biased eye of the person who created it. I once asked three different people who claimed to be able enter the Halls of Akasha as easily as my local library, if they could tell me where 'Dion Fortune' first went to school. I wasn't testing them, but as they were boasting to me of their abilities at the time I thought it worth a punt, as I really did (and do) want to know this. Of course I got three varying answers, all of them pitched toward their own concerns and none of them – as far as I could judge - with any useful substance or even likelihood. Meanwhile...

I was startled this morning when, looking for a completely unrelated document in the bottom of my wardrobe, I found a very old Diary of mine in which the Magickal Name I used then was *Sùil Air Ais*. I had no knowledge of the Gaelic, and had simply seen the phrase in a since forgotten book about the Highlands that told me it meant 'Looking Backward', and felt that this expressed something of my essence then.

I think we all have those moments of revelation when we realise that unimportant and perhaps irrelevant impulses, ideas and events from decades earlier take on exquisite meaning. This is the First Swirlings again. Of course, as William G. Gray enjoined, you should NEVER reveal your Magickal Name to ANYONE. He often spoke in block capitals. But that fella inwardly known to himself alone as *Sùil Air Ais* was from long ago, and the inner moniker I use now has long since supplanted that one and the others that followed. I do remember dropping *Sùil Air Ais* because it reminded me too much of the acronym for South African Airlines. Still, it startled me that perhaps Suil, or Sulis, even before I knew she existed, was putting her teaspoon into my cup and beginning to stir it.

The Romans linked her firmly with Minerva, so that the temple became known as that of Sulis-Minerva. The fact that they retained her name and indeed used it to precede that of their own national goddess meant that they recognised her importance. So what do we know about Minerva and also Brigid? – for they and Sulis all flow and swirl together and I'm not sure we can easily separate them.

Minerva was primarily the goddess of wisdom, and was accredited with inventing spinning, weaving, commerce, numbers and music. She was so multi-talented that Ovid described her as the 'Goddess of a thousand works'. The gilt bronze head of her that can still be seen  today in the Roman Baths was actually found by archaeologists in the sewers. They felt that it had been deliberately damaged in the centuries after her worship had died or gone underground in that area. Her sacred symbols are the owl, the snake, and the olive tree. Solinus, writing in his 'Collectanea rerum memorabilium' in the late third century, noted that in the temple of Minerva in Bath a perpetual fire was kept which '...never whitens to ash, but as the flame fades turns into rocky lumps.' This may well have been caused by the use of local Somerset coal which, when burnt, became cinders which were found on the site the better part of two thousand years later.

Bridgid/Brigit/Brig was a goddess of pre-Christian Ireland, and associated with Spring, fertility, healing, smithing, poetry, cattle, serpents and sacred wells. Elsewhere she was known as the Goddess  of the Hearth-fire, which perhaps has echoes of the perpetual fire once kept burning in the Temple of Sulis. Even into the Christian era, nineteen nuns at Kildare once tended a perpetual flame for Saint Brigid, whose attributes are exactly the same as that for the goddess. The late hereditary witch Paddy Slade told me that it was usually nine priestesses used in such places: three to tend the fire, three to go gathering or creating the combustible materials, and the other three resting until it was their turn to be active. Brigid seems to have made a seamless flow through early Christianity and then back into the devotional aspects of modern paganism without losing any parts of herself.

When you – anyone – starts to look into the nature of any goddess it becomes hard to disengage. For example, it is almost impossible for me just to dip into Robert Graves' *The White Goddess* because I get swept away with all the currents I glimpse. But perhaps we all have got within ourselves an area like the Crack in the Temple of Sulis, from where powerful currents emerge: plus connected places wherein we keep our own perpetual fires burning, with various bits of our psyches working in shifts to maintain them, often without us realising. I could probably spend this whole journal babbling about other aspects of the Temple of Sulis, such as the Roman images of Luna, who might be another aspect of Sulis, and all sorts of druidy notions involving water and serpents and caves that can be glimpsed at this one spot. Not to mention the magnificent face of what *might* be the sun-god Bel, who was perhaps regarded as heating the waters. But as our concern involves springs, wells and ponds in this area that we may imagine as falling under the spell of Sulis, then we must part company with the Roman Baths for a little while and see where we feel compelled to travel.

The Roman Temple of Sulis Minerva

Chapter 2

In one drop of water are found all the secrets of all the oceans; in one aspect of You are found all the aspects of existence.

Kahlil Gibran

It's Valentine's Day today and we have a meal booked at an Italian restaurant in Bradford on Avon. Considering the amount of time Minerva has spent within my head these past few days I think that's vaguely appropriate. I fully expect the waitress to be a priestess of her Mysteries and will leave an adequate tip when we've finished.

But Margaret has told me that two things happen whenever I start writing about anything magickal:

1. I get ill, with a high and spasmodic fever
2. I have dreams of celebrities who chat to me about the most banal things.

When the latter happens I believe that it is an attempt being made by my mind to bridge the gap between normal consciousness and the supra-normal. These dream images, however glamorous, should not be taken at their face value. I think that in earlier times, long before the printing press, books and newspapers or any form of electronic media, people would have dreams of Saints and pass these on as divine communications. Perhaps they were, but the same people today now have dreams of David Bowie, or Michael Jackson or the King himself – Elvis – and churn out a load of tosh. For me, the 'celebrities' that I dream about are all living and the one I dreamt about when writing *The Templar Door* was Prince Harry. A nice lad, but do I believe that it was really him gadding about on the astral? Absolutely not. The celebrities who came to me in my dreams when I began this project were Sting and his wife Trudie Style; even as they were speaking my dream-self was aware that they weren't saying anything that wasn't already in my mind, and so I woke up.

Well, pause here. Today is the 15th February and I spent last night in the spare room, so as not to wake Margaret with my snotting and snorting. We had to cancel the meal at the Italian restaurant because I don't think the fellow diners would have appreciated the trumpet solos (with strings) that I was playing through my nose.

But when I went to bed I pulled the curtains in the room back and watched the waxing moon move across the window, hoping that Luna might do the magick carpet thing and whisk my astral off through the Celestial Gate into bright realms.

Perhaps she did. I had an intense dream of meeting a cheery community who lived in a hidden valley in an alternate realm. This was not a mountainous Thibetan, Shangri-la sort of place, but somewhere hilly, lush, green and Western European. The entrance to the valley was just ahead and I dearly wanted to go there but they were ganged amicably before it, wanting to know more about me. Instead I found myself questioning *them*:

Do you know of Jesus? I asked, unaccountably, and they seemed genuinely ignorant, at which I felt pleased. The older ones puckered their brows as if I'd mentioned a fabled person they had once heard of at the edges of their myths.

That's all. When I woke I did have the feeling that I'd been drawn close to a parallel – or do I mean alternate? - realm where things and their histories were somewhat different to ours. I'd have liked it there. I'm sure it would have had lots of springs and small waterfalls and a clear river down its length. It was intensely real during the dream; perhaps some of my readers have been there too?

Then I got up and looked out the back window over our garden, hoping for appropriate omens that might relate to Sulis or Minerva, such as owls or serpents, but there was only a menacing and monstrously fat pigeon perched on top of our clothes pole seemingly keeping all the small wild birds away from the feeders. I wanted to call him El Chapo. Margaret wanted to call him Prince Albert. I pointed out that this is the name given to a certain procedure that some men do with heavy metal rings and their willies, and so we settled on the name Prince instead.

I'll let you know if and when this ever becomes relevant. But at that very moment I got a text from a lady who found that she was related to Humphrey de Bohun, former Baron of Trowbridge in the 12 Century, whose descendant may have been one of the last Templars in Wiltshire.

'Not the bloody Templars again!' cried Margaret, for they had wearied us both exceedingly when they had encamped within my head and our house during most of last summer.

'No, it's holy wells we're after. Wells and springs and ponds and picnicks!'

You'll notice I use the letter 'k' here. Hence: magic**k**, music**k** and picnic**k**. Aleister Crowley had a long, learned explanation for this terminal letter being a reference to the *kteis*, which is (he assures us) a Greek word for the vagina. In one way the uses this to distinguish the High Magick he practised from the mere stage Magic of the conjuror. For him, it also implied undercurrents of the Sex Magick fundamental to his Ordo Templi Orientis.

Personally I rather like the arcane look of the words magick and musick and I'm not suggesting there will be any occult hank-panky during our picnicks. But it was the very real Adept known as Christine Hartley who pointed out that on inner levels, during the interchange of energies between a priest and his priestess, *all* magic is sex magick. I'm quoting off the top of my head now but somewhere in the joint Diaries of her and Kim Seymour that I published as *Dancers to the Gods*, the latter wrote: 'I *drove* the energy over to her, and she drew it from me.' As Christine said, they were never lovers, never so much as snogged, but during their Work they exchanged very powerful currents that were entirely magic**k**al.

And I think that in a subtle way something of this sort goes on within the countryside when you're linked – however gently and subtly - with Nature. So I'm rather hoping that when the better weather comes and the magnificent English Spring arrives, our picnicks will involve more than just ham and cheese sandwiches and fizzy drinks.

The only problem I have at the moment is in trying to escape (though temporarily) from what I might call the Sulian whirlpool. I think that if she had her way I'd still be within her temple, still writing about the myriad wonders that keep surging into my mind even as I write. But I'm determined to resume my original project and visit the local wells and springs that served the larger community of Wiltshire, not just the elite who visited Aquae Sulis in order to proposition her as if she were some kind of hedge-fund manager who might make their fortunes through invisible investment.

This is a problem that everyone experiences when they, accidentally or otherwise, find themselves within the flow of inner plane energies. The contact can be so strong that everything else is often dropped, and they can end up causing chaos and dancing through their life as one half of the Blue Brothers, on a mission for God, convinced that the world will suffer if they don't follow this to the Source. But they never quite get there, and everything stops overnight, and they are just left feeling rather wet and confused and with a vague realisation that 'Mystery will always remain', as some medium once said.

Believe me, I speak from experience. I have often been swirled into areas I wouldn't otherwise have chosen, didn't even know existed, in order do what I felt was 'Their' work. I wouldn't say that these vortices were Black Holes – quite the opposite – but they made me determined not to become a kind of spiritual flotsam buffeted by powers.

So I'm determined to break free of Sulis, just for a little while, and get out on the roads of Wiltshire to see those smaller upwellings of Water that were just as important to the common folk who used them.

Besides, call me a miser if you like, but at £32 a visit to the Roman Baths, I just had to find a cheaper alternative. And forget that tosh about the 32 Paths of the Tree of Life I mentioned earlier: I uprooted the Kabbalah from my psyche decades ago and have never regretted it.

Now, at this moment in the last week of February, I just have to get to Cat's Well.

Our area has a number of wells and springs with 'sacred' connotations that are now long forgotten. Just off the top of my head there are Ela's Well, the Shingle Bell Well, Conkwell and a couple of Ladywells - all within a very short drive from Trowbridge. Many of them are little more than cracks in the ground, or gaps in a wall where the water trickles out and sometimes fills a trough. In the days before horses were made redundant as a mode of transport for the wealthy, you would find horse troughs in almost every small village.

Yet when I use the term 'well' you've probably got an image in your mind of a round brick structure with a little roof above it and a winch to lower a bucket. I think most of the English-speaking world is familiar with the old Nursery Rhyme about Jack and Jill. We all know it, and we all visualise the red-bricked structure as we chant:

Jack and Jill
Went up the hill
To fetch a pail of water
Jack fell down
And broke his crown,
And Jill came tumbling after.

Curiously, the rhyme described a real hill, and a real person who once lived at the bottom of it, though whether old Dame Dob really did patch someone's head with vinegar and brown paper as described in the second verse will never be known. This is at Kilmersdon Hill, only a few miles from us. We've never been, but climbing that hill and finding that source of Water while chanting the rhyme and invoking both our own childhoods and those of half the western world will be on our itinerary over the next few months.

But while I'm at it, conscious that I'm doing the equivalent of being trapped in an eddy, I might say something about my use of the term Water with a capital Wuh before I finally set off for Cat's Well.

My first title for this book was going to be *The Memory of Water*, but apparently this is also the name of a play currently running in London's West End. Then I toyed with calling it *Amniosis,* which is an entirely contrived (by me!) and somewhat awkward term meant to evoke something of the amniotic fluids from which we all came. I do think that Water means more than just the liquid we can get from a tap or springing from the ground, just as the Waters from the Gap are more than just a hot outpouring with varying uses when held in various containers. After all Water has long been seen as a symbol of the Unconscious Mind. And the Unconscious Mind, as some magicians feel, is synonymous with the 'rolling billows of the astral plane'. So if you know what you're doing (and I usually don't), then you can access all sorts of levels via this medium.

I'll come back to this notion of the magickal memory of Water later, but if you've got this far in our book, then you'll know exactly what I mean and be making your own inner connections.

Cat's Well, in Bratton, is little more than a square cavity in a high wall by the roadside. Two stone steps lead down to the well which is filled with water issuing from a narrow pipe. It is easily missed and we had passed it several times without knowing exactly where to look. This time we parked on the narrow road and found it straight away.

We did have an odd encounter just before the well which quite startled me. Some years ago I wrote a novel called *Twisted Light* which was set largely in this valley, about a young disabled man called Kaspar O'Malley who had talents for Remote Viewing. In his last years, supported by his three carers, he returns here and tries (unsuccessfully) to buy the Mill House. As we approached Cat's Well we met a bent, frail, very old man in a wheelchair with three carers. He smiled at me hugely as they went past, as if we were old friends.

That's Kaspar O'Malley! I whispered to Margaret in astonishment. She agreed. The old chap was exactly as we had always seen him.

Of course, it was NOT Kaspar. Kaspar didn't exist except in my own creative imagination. He was not based upon anyone I knew, other than expressing some aspects of my own character. If I had been bold enough or rude enough to chat to the fellow, there would have been a perfectly reasonable and local explanation for his presence there. But somehow, for the purposes of manifesting myth at a magickal spot, I met up with an echo of my own inner faery tales.

This will be exquisitely relevant when I come to talk more about the various energies and entities that can impinge upon us at certain times and places. Meanwhile, I just *had* to get some water from the well...

Did we use 'barbarous Names of Power' and call upon Nixsa, who in the system of magick used in Victorian times, was known as Lord of the Element Water, residing under the jurisdiction of the Archangel Gabriel? No, I might have done in the past but I'm after simpler stuff in these End Times of both myself and the world. *Hello,* was all we

both said when we got there.

Cat's Well seemed rather sad and neglected. There was only a small pipe from which water dripped rather than trickled or flowed. At the base was about 6 inches of water, clogged with dead leaves and other mulch. I should have cleared this out, but decided to do that another time.

Perhaps this was a metaphor for something either within me or the world at large? I'll have to think about that one.

I scooped up some water into a bottle and then used a little device marked TDS for measuring water quality. This registered as 25.4 ppm. I don't know what either TDS stands for or ppm, but I understand that when our tap water at home [which shows as 23.6] is filtered through our special jug, it then registers as 00.0, which is apparently good.

I could get swirled away in my yarn here, because after I'd taken the water from Cat's Well we then decided to find Luccombe Springs. Although they lie nearby, their only access until recently was through the grounds of Luccombe Manor, owned at the moment by a pal of Prince Harry who didn't like strangers in boots and geeky walking gear stomping with attitude through his property. Margaret, being far bolder than I, insisted that we take a cunning route around his place and across some nearby fields and so we found ourselves in, we can only call it... faeryland.

This place is enchanted, she whispered, not wanting to spoil the atmosphere within the glade. And it was. The waters from Salisbury Plain raged out of an orifice in low brickwork, pooling crystal clear and running off in streams. Here was purity and clarity on all levels and my silly little machine registered them at 00.0.

Wow... she said, and I said nowt.

But if I start talking about Lucca now we'll never get into the Mysteries of Katherine and how she might be a continuation of Sulis/Minerva/Bride. And besides I don't want anyone else *ever* to go there.

For me, the important thing about Cat's Well is its name, which as a I said earlier is a contraction of St. Catherine's Well. For some reason St Catherine was an enormously important figure in this particular area of Wiltshire and surrounds, although now largely forgotten. To expand:

Saint Catherine of Alexandria, or Saint Katharine of Alexandria, was supposedly born in 287 CE and was the greatest of the women saints of the old Egyptian church. The name Katharine means 'pure' or 'clear' and I can't help thinking this relates to that Gaelic 'soilleir' of similar meaning. There are numerous other Saints called Catherine or Katharine but this one definitely refers specifically to Katharine of Alexandria because her Saint's Day, November 25th, was the most important day in the religious calendar for the peoples of this area in Wiltshire. They called it Cattern's Day, celebrated it with special cattern cakes, named wells and springs and alms houses after her, and up until the 19th Century they regarded this as a far more important day than Christmas. She was also known as Saint Catherine of the Wheel because of the device that Maxentius supposedly used to kill her, but I think that something else is going on here. Later, I'll show you what I think the wheel actually was, and how it flowed into the collective unconscious of the peoples in this particular area.

But without getting too swirled and whirled, I've just noted that within an arrow's flight from Cat's Well was the Priory of the Bonshommes, with its chantry dedicated to St Katherine the 'Pure One'. I can't help but think that the *bonshommes* or the 'Good Men' of Cathar fame have their own stories from this area that might need telling some day.

However, any attempt to find historical evidence of Katharine of Alexandria, the patron Saint of spinners, lace-makers, rope-makers and spinsters, inevitably takes me toward the very real figure of Hypatia of Alexandria. In fact a number of scholars argue that the story of the former was taken from actual events within the life of the latter.

Just briefly looking into Hypatia's story it's clear that she was a major figure in her own lifetime who could be a prime candidate for becoming one of the subtly intrusive Inner Plane Adeptii beloved of certain Traditions. An Egyptian Coptic Bishop called John of Niki was the author of a Chronicle extending from Adam to the end of the Muslim conquest of Egypt. In his jaundiced account he wrote of Hypatia:

And in those days there appeared in Alexandria a female philosopher, a pagan named Hypatia, and she was devoted at all times to magic, astrolabes and instruments of music, and she beguiled many people through her Satanic wiles. And the governor of the city honoured her exceedingly; for she had beguiled him through her magic. And he ceased attending church as had been his custom... And he not only did this, but he drew many believers to her, and he himself received the unbelievers at his house.

At the time of her death in 415 CE she was seen as the world's leading mathematician and astronomer, the only woman for whom such a claim can be made. If anyone might seem to be an avatar of Minerva then Hypatia fits the bill. She was also a popular teacher and lecturer on philosophical topics of such a nature that she was seen as a Pagan at a time of bitter conflict between varying brands of Christianity and Jews. Mainly she was concerned with an approach to the One, putting her into the flow of the Gnostic currents for which Alexandria was famous. (Personally, if I had to sum up my own beliefs it would be through the simple Gnostic statement *All is One*. Which might be simple, but believe me it often ain't easy.)

Hypatia, like Katharine, took a vow a to remain a virgin despite the many contemporaries who seem to have drooled over her beauty. Like Katharine, she was tortured to death but in her case it was by Christians.

I know I'm about to sound offensive, but the hard-core Christians in those days were not much different to the present-day followers of Daesh. Convert or die (preferably in the most horrible of ways) was their theme. Up until then, Alexandria was a multi-cultural, multi-faith melting-pot, the centre of Gnostic philosophies which had (and have) a great influence upon the world. Did the Christians (who also burned the great libraries at Alexandria) create the phantasm of Katharine to hide what they did to Hypatia?

I think I'll stop here. Hypatia is becoming a distraction. You might want to chase her up yourselves and see where she will lead. Despite the obvious parallels between the lives of the two figures, I'm going to work from the premise that Katharine *did* exist, and that those parallels are more explained by Hypatia being what Timothy Leary called a 'continuation' of a cosmic script, rather than a reincarnation or legendary reclamation by Christian spin-doctors.

You see I have to confess to a sense of bewilderment at this very moment, so let me try and explain and also apologise for this journey of mine among the Wells not being a linear one...

I woke a few nights ago remembering a small pamphlet that I had stumbled upon over 20 years ago in the Wiltshire Archives, with the unlikely title of *Isis and Nephthys in Wiltshire and Elsewhere*. I'd been intrigued – though not totally convinced – by the authors' premise that the area around Bradford on Avon, Holt and Great Chalfield (all just a few miles from us) held traces of the worship of these twin goddesses. I had no thought that this might relate to the present project but as I've long since learned to go along with unlikely impulses, I knew that I had to read it again. The only surviving copy of this little booklet of only 23 pages, written in 1938 by Rendel Harris and E.F. Wills, can still be seen there and they kindly sent me a photocopy, which arrived yesterday.[v]

Nephthys   Isis

I needn't go into detail but my jaw dropped to see their argument that in 1170 St Catherine (whom they see as an echo of the Isis worship from Egypt), was patroness of the City of Bath. Indeed, in the fifteenth century, the citizen had to take an oath at his admission to the freedom of the city, that he would keep St Catherine's Day as a holy day yearly. The Hospital of St Catherine, built by two sisters whom Harris argues were really a folk-memory of Isis and Nephthys, was situated in Bilbury Lane, behind the present day Thermae Spa, which still uses Sulis' waters.

Can we say that Sulis flows through Minerva and also into Katharine? This must be the case. Minerva was credited with inventing spinning and weaving, while Katharine was, among other things, patron saint of spinners and weavers. I hope to get greater clarity over the weeks to come as we track down the Waters within other nearby Wells, including the Ladywell and Bride Springs near Cat's Well.

I begin to see now that the thoughts and small happenings that can occur in travelling to such places are just as important as any revelations that might arise in getting there. Although there was not much to see about Cat's Well on the outer level, you can appreciate that behind the thin trickle of water there was actually a powerful current of Water on other levels.

It's funny, but all I wanted a couple of weeks ago was to get some water from a well to put in our garden pond. Now it seems that I'm getting Water from a Well and don't quite know how to contain it.

I'm not complaining.

Young Violet Firth, on the cusp of becoming 'Dion Fortune', came to Bath to give some talks in the early part of the 20th Century. Her parents, Arthur and Jenny, met courted and married in neighbouring Limpley Stoke, and her maternal grandparents John and Elizabeth Smith ran the state-of-the-art (for that era) Hydropathic Establishment in that small village. The name explains it all: the use of water for healing and rejuvenation.

As I said earlier I had always assumed that it was this connection that brought me down to Bath and its immediate surrounds, until I began to dwell upon Sulis and co. and started to think that other energies might be afoot. And I do rather think in terms of Katherine or Sulis or Brigid being flowing 'energies' rather than 'entities' in the spirit sense.

So... is there a whorl of consciousness – a magickal current if you like - on the inner planes answering to St. Katharine and nudging me along now? I would say Yes.

I don't doubt the existence of what some call Guides, not to mention Masters, Ascended Masters, Mahatmas, Devas and all the angelic and archangelic hierarchies that people call upon and connect with. But I think our attitude toward them might need re-adjusting. In child-like (but not necessarily childish) terms they exist on *different* levels to us, but these are not necessarily *superior* levels. They might have a *higher* level of vibration, to use the old Spiritualist terminology, but I would argue that this is not in any way *superior.* I much prefer the magicians' term of 'inner contacts', when used to describe these beings.

When 'Dion Fortune' was in full flow and bringing through the teachings she later published as the *Cosmic Doctrine,* there was one extremely important observation made by one of her Masters:

> The Masters as you picture them are all 'imagination'. Note well that I did not say the Masters were imagination: I said 'The Masters as you picture them...' What we are you cannot realise and it is a waste of time to try to do so, but you can imagine us on the astral plane and we can contact you through your imagination, and although your mental picture is not real or actual, the results of it are real and actual.

This is of crucial importance, and can give clarity to what goes on when you find yourself swept along by any magickal current. The energies of Sulis may well take shape as Minerva, Bridey or Katharine. They may uses images on the astral plane that act like icons on a modern touch-screen. But the crucial statement, as far as I'm concerned here is: ' What we are you cannot realise and it is a waste of time to try to do so...' Well, I wouldn't *quite* say it's a waste of time trying to make sense of all these energies: for me it's extremely invigorating, hence I'm typing this out at 3 a.m. because I can't sleep after our visit to Cat's Well and the Luccombe Springs.

Then again, because I'm retired I don't have to worry about sleepless nights followed by a long hard day at work, as used to be the case.

But I do accept that, in the heart of the vortex, it may never be possible for me to completely grasp 'what they are'. When the major adept 'Gareth Knight' commented upon this in a different context, he suggested that Inner Plane communicators can often use the images of personalities to create a convenient 'mock-up' as a means to enable two-way contact.

Perhaps they also use the images of places to do the same?

There were two other sites very near Cat's Well that we needed to visit but I might go by myself next week while Margaret is in Brussels. She seems to have a knack for finding lost wells and springs and stops me getting pixie-led in the search for them. Well, either it's a case of me getting confounded by uncanny sprites attached to the Land, or maybe I'm just a crap map-reader.

These sites are: the Ladywell somewhere in Edington and Bridewell Springs that lie below the scoured hillside-image of the Bratton White Horse, the high point of what we regard as 'our kingdom'.

(When I mention 'our kingdom' we define it as everything we can see from Westbury White Horse, which takes in Frome to the West (if you know where to look), the edges of Bath to the North and Solsbury Hill (which we'll have to visit given the name), and points to the far east, that will just about include the area around the Broad Well if I jump up and down on a clear day. The south is largely hidden and is a military training ground anyway.)

The exact location of the Ladywell bewilders me no matter how carefully I look at the Ordnance Survey map references, Google Maps and even dear old Google Earth. I'll let you know how I get on as I try to find it without my own Lady next to me, and hope I don't end up in Straw Dog territory.

Plus I'm rather hoping that the Bridewell Springs might have echoes of what we found next to the church at Alton Priors, when we were working on *The Templar Door*. Here there is a bubbling pond known as the *Broad* Well, consisting of two spring-fed pools each flowing into separate springs which eventually converge. At different places, small bubbles break away from the bottom of the crystal clear water and perturb the surface. These are apparently caused by air being released from the local chalk aquifer up into the pools. The water there will eventually flow past the ancient sites of Marden, Durrington Walls and Stonehenge.

Onward...

Chapter 3

[It] can scald you or freeze you. In the presence of certain organic molecules it can form carbonic acids so nasty that they can strip the leaves from trees and eat the faces off statuary. In bulk, when agitated, it can strike with a fury that no human edifice could withstand. Even for those who have learned to live with it, it is an often murderous substance. We call it water.

Bill Bryson *A Short History of Nearly Everything*

I'm scribbling this in a note pad in a cafe in Frome. It's another freakishly bright and warm day in this last week of February. Apparently it's hotter here than in Athens. I'm thinking of opening a travel agency there so that the Greeks can come and get some winter sun.

Frome, incidentally, is a strange, alternative, higgledy-piggledy and in places quite beautiful little town with odd energies flowing through some of the ancient streets. I'm here alone because M is in Brussels so I thought I'd come and track down remnants of St Katharine. Some years ago I'd come across a wee snippet in some pamphlet (since forgotten) which said that she was the saint to whom the old town was originally dedicated. I climbed the hill to the massive church of St John the Baptist and hoped to find her lurking up there, but no luck. Apparently there's a statue of her on the north side, behind locked gates and not accessible to the public or visible from the street.

Coming back to the centre, down the narrow Cheap Street which is lined with unusual and artisan shops I criss-crossed the rapid stream which runs down its length (no more than six inches wide and deep) which descends from the church where Katharine is hiding. Whenever I've done this I've had the sense that this criss-cross movement over the stream was somehow cleansing my aura. Try it yourselves and let me know.

I'm being prophetic and perhaps a bit bolshie now but I predict that in a couple of generations the sort of folk who now gravitate to

Glastonbury will instead come to Frome. The front-runners are there already! And this will upset the Avalonians no end but I loved the detailed analysis in Graham Phillips' *The Marian Conspiracy* which shows that the very first writings about 'Avalon' could not possibly have related to Glastonbury and could only have pointed to what we now call Anglesey.

Yesterday we should have gone to the Ladywell and the Bridewell Springs as planned. But we've found that the whorls of Sulis are apt to snatch us up and carry us off in different directions. And so we went to Jack and Jill's Hill instead, which we hadn't planned to visit until the end of this piece of Work. For the curious, Jack was a real person who had been killed by a falling stone in a nearby quarry. His wife Jill was pregnant at the time and later gave birth to a son but died not long afterwards. Villagers raised the boy as 'Jill's son', and apparently there are families called Gilson in this area today who are descendants.

Basically we were still having the sublime weather that will get into the record books. It would have been a crime against the marital state and human loving not to have a picnick.

You will all know the Nursery Rhyme, I expect, so say it to yourselves now while remembering being tiny, and conjure up the images you did then. The reality of the place is this...

In a small, story-book sort of village amid the rambling lanes of Somerset, there is a story-book narrow paved path which leads very steeply up a story-book hill. On the way up the hill there are various carved stones which give the lines from the rhyme. Then visualise the sort of story-book Victorian school you might expect to find at the top of this, standing there alone, with a story-book wishing well next to it.

We were both deeply moved at the top, and it being half-term there was no-one else there. It is still a working junior school and the children walk up and down the hill every day during term. The well is actually deep and real, even though it looks story-book, but the top has long since been sealed off to stop the children throwing teachers and other objects down it.

You see the thing about wells and springs and water sources is that they are all, in some ways, connected with the communities who used them, and thus – in the broad sense – our Ancestors.

Wherever you are now as you read this, remember back to your childhoods and the link with your parents and, if you are lucky, the warm and safe moments when they chanted this rhyme to you with unconditional love. Or if you were damaged by useless parents (and god knows there are enough of them) then invoke the could-have-beens and should-have-beens and try not to cry.

Margaret and I, silently, summoned up our own childhoods. We quietly invoked our parents by the Holy Names of Mum and Dad and then chanted the rhyme as we looked out over the rolling hills of Somerset.

I would explain that although Margaret is cosmopolitan, much-travelled and internationalist in outlook after having lived in Russia, Holland and Belgium, she is actually a Hampshire lass, and spent her early years in Portsmouth where her Dad was an engineer in the Royal Navy. Yet although she was brought up in the far south of England and I from the coal-mining communities of the far north, we both had this nursery rhyme as a common link.

I must admit that when we walked down the hill I felt a bit like Moses coming down from the mountain, but instead of the 10 Commandments blazing in my mind I had the sense of making things in my own childhood a little bit clearer. I think my face might have shone.

The massive church at the bottom of the hill, dedicated to Saints Peter and Paul, I think, was open. *Gaudete* was playing inside. I only know that tune coz it was a hit in the 70s by the folk-rock band 'Steeleye Span'. They were filming something for the Deanery, whatever that is, but they offered us tea and cake as we sat in the pews. The lovely lady who served us didn't know that I was a Master of the Occult on a picnick with his Shakti; I doubt if she would have cared.

I'm not getting *too* far away from Sulis here. If the well at the top of the hill had been unsealed I would have dropped coins into it. During the Roman era people came from far and wide to drop things into Her waters. Many of them were in fact curses, or maledictions, a reminder that not all Goddess worship was soft and cuddly.

Many of the wishes were written, sometimes in reverse, in British Latin, on what seemed to be thin lead sheets. Lead was important to the Romans and readily expressed such needs for revenge, just as diamonds today echo other feelings. They also used drops of molten lead into cold water as a means of augury, in much the same way that we used to do until recently with tea leaves. Some of the curses or pleas, even now, capture the agonies of the supplicants:

> Solinus to the goddess Sulis Minerva. I give to your divinity and majesty my bathing tunic and cloak. Do not allow sleep or health to him who has done me wrong, whether man or woman or whether slave or free unless he reveals himself and brings those goods to your temple.

Then there is the unusual example that began with the words 'Whether pagan or Christian' which shows that Bath was a melting pot of religions and cultures in that era:

> Whether pagan or Christian, whether man or woman, whether boy or girl, whether slave or free whoever has stolen from me, Annianus , son of Matutina, six silver coins from my purse, you, Lady Goddess, are to exact them from him. If through some deceit he has given me...and do not give thus to him but reckon as (?) the blood of him who has invoked his upon me.

With others you can almost feel their anger 1700 years later, and it's a surprisingly modern sense of outrage:

> May he who carried off Vilbia from me become liquid as the water. May she who so obscenely devoured her become dumb.

> ...so long as someone, whether slave or free, keeps silent or knows anything about it, he may be accursed in (his) blood, and eyes and every limb and even have all his intestines quite eaten away if he has stolen the ring or been privy (to the theft).

> Docimedis has lost two gloves and asks that the thief responsible should lose their minds and eyes in the goddess' temple.

I think I might have become good pals with Docimedis.

There are many others, most of them inscribed with the letters *DSM* or the words *Deae Sulis Minerva* which shows that they were dedicated to the goddess Sulis Minerva. Some of them may well have been organised or directed by the in-house Haruspex. An haruspex was a person trained to practice a form of divination called haruspicy: the inspection of the entrails of sacrificed animals, especially the livers of sacrificed sheep and poultry. The altar he dedicated to Sulis read: 'To the goddess Sul, Lucius Marcus, a grateful Haruspex, donated out of his devotion'. This is the only evidence we have of a priest in Britain who practised divination in this way.

In other curses names are mentioned and this is where we get to the meaty stuff:

> I have given to the goddess Sulis the six silver coins which I have lost. It is for the goddess to exact [them] from the names written below: Senicianus and Saturninus and Anniola.

It may well be that Lucius Marcus Memor, as he is also called, advised the supplicants as to technique, as the inscriptions tended to follow the same formula. First, the stolen property is declared as having been transferred to a deity so that the loss becomes the deity's loss; the suspect is named and, in 21 cases, so is the victim; the victim then asks the deity to visit afflictions on the thief (including death) not as a punishment but to induce the thief to hand the stolen items back.

As one commentator noted, it's almost as though this formula was taken from a handbook. Personally I think there may a market for this today: *An Idiot's Guide to Cursing* perhaps?

But it wasn't just curses that were flung into the depths of Sulis' waters; archaeologists also found 34 beautifully engraved gemstones.

 The person who sacrificed them must have been desperate for some divine response, and also confident that he or she would get one.

This act of throwing things into the waters was not just a practice exclusive to Aquae Sulis. Lakes and rivers throughout Britain and Europe where the Celts held sway have yielded, not curses as such, but actual treasures. The dried-up lake bed of Llyn Cerrig Bach in Anglesey (the true Avalon), revealed a hoard of over a hundred and fifty objects of bronze and iron. Workmen discovered these objects whilst digging peat from the site of the former lake's edge. The collection included seven swords, six spearheads, fragments of a shield, part of a bronze trumpet, two gang chains, fragments of iron wagon tyres and horse gear, blacksmith's tools, fragments of two cauldrons, iron bars for trading and animal bones. These items were once thrown into a lake that must have been sacred to the Druids before the Romans wiped them out on Anglesey. Our modern urge to throw coins into a well and make a wish seems to be a continuation of this.

The obvious question is, did Sulis answer the pleas? Did the wretch who stole Docimedis' gloves lose his mind and eyes? Can deities step in and either help or blast?

It's an old saying that whoever curses, is cursed, and I go along with that. Although I've never used the full monty of Bell, Book and Candle or yet fashioned curses on folded lead sheets to implore the help of Sulis Minerva, I've flung inner currents of spleen and venom at any number of people over the years whom I felt deserved it. Only once did it ever work and even now I don't regret it. Most of the time, however, it rather withered me.

I did meet a witch once who apparently had a great reputation for blasting people. Those in the know called her Mort. I don't know where she is now and I don't really want to meet her as she talked far too much and I couldn't get a word in edgewise.

I know a couple of people who have thrown coins into a beautiful little well in Bradford on Avon and assured me that their wishes were granted. I'll put this to a mild test in the next few days and although I won't tell you what I wish for, I will tell you if it worked.

Years ago, Margaret and I made our way with great difficulty to a lake near Betwys y Coed in Snowdonia, encountering bizarre twists and turns that made an otherwise simple hike extremely unpleasant. The lake (or llyn in Welsh) was beautiful, still, deserted. I was about to skim a silver coin into it (silver for Moon, or gold pound-coins for Sun) when it became clear to both of us that the lake just did not want us there. Don't know why. We didn't argue and left immediately. Haven't been since.

Likewise, there is no way that I would drop any coins or any precious items into the waters of Luccombe's Pond.

But if you do want to try something safe and simple then find some local bridge with water running underneath. Look over the side where the river runs *away* from you. Summon up in your mind all those things about yourself and your life that you want to get rid of. Then spit into the water and visualise these dissolving, perhaps adding: *Sulis, take these away..* Once you've done that, go to the other side of the bridge and watch the river flowing *toward* you. Summon up up all those good, healthy, loving things that you now want brought into your life and likewise spit into the river, saying *Sulis, bring these to me*. Imagine yourself in future when they come to you: as if by magick.

This does work, honest. But don't expect it to be quick.

After our trip to the Jack and Jill Hill we still had a whole afternoon of perfect weather ahead of us. Without any sense of irony Margaret suggested we take our picnick to the nearby town of Wells.

Wells in Somerset, not far from the Las Vegas of Glastonbury, is a small town that is technically regarded as being a city, because of the presence of its stupendous cathedral. It gets its name from three wells dedicated to Saint Andrew: one in the market place, and two within the grounds of the Bishop's Palace. We sat in the sun next to the moat and watched the swans. There is a bell on the wall of the Palace which they have learned to pull and get food from a man who will pop his head out of the window. I assured Margaret that I have seen this happen but I've probably created a false memory.

I like swans. In my next life I want to be swan and mate for life and have the Bishop of Bath and Wells come to the window and feed me. I'll be nicer to him than I've been to the Fisher King.

And while I'm on the topic of swans I would add now that Andrew Collins makes a watertight case for the Great Pyramids matching up **not** with the three stars on Orion's Belt (one of them is slightly awry) but the crucial stars of Cygnus where the match is perfect.[vi] And while I rant on, Philip Coppens also shows that Osiris was **not** the constellation of Orion, with Sirius, (Isis), at his heel like a little puppy. Osiris was seen by the ancient Egyptians as the star

Canopus, the second brightest in the sky, only viewable from a certain latitude. Seen from those levels, Sirius and Canopus dance in the heavens perfectly, in balance, and the people of Khem would have known this.[vii]

These things are important. If we now know the truth about Jack and Jill, we must be able to say the same about Osiris and Isis. This will come in handy some day, I feel sure.

The monstrously beautiful and awesome Wells Cathedral would take at least a book for me to do it justice. Instead, for this piece of Work, I just need to mention that we went inside into the 'Quiet Place' dedicated to St Katharine.

We sat quietly, that's all. I said the things in my head to Katharine I needed to say. I don't know what was in M's lovely mind but our silence was companionable and most people in all their long lives, never get to experience this. So I also said a big Thank You.

Which brings me to a jolly useful teaching point for this stage of our Search...

When you get involved in your own magickal workings you necessarily want to use the 'sonics', if I might call them that: the Words of Power. Which is an extraordinarily seductive concept. Today, we can open doors, phones, computers and turn lights on by voice-recognition software that responds to individual words and tones. In my early days of learning magick (entirely via books and snail-mail correspondence with the likes of William G. Gray, W. E. Butler, Kenneth Grant, and a host of others) I assumed that such words as I had learned were made effective by volume and intensity. On the occasions when Dad was at the Working Man's Social Club and Mam at the Bingo, our sitting room would echo with *Yod he Vau Heh! Adonai! Eheieh! Agla!* as I performed the delicious Banishing Ritual of the Pentagram. Gawd knows what the neighbou*rs* on either side thought as they tried to watch *Rawhide or Bonanza*. I had no idea what these sonics actually meant and was quite dismayed when I saw them translated. I think my Banishings lost a little power then.

Likewise, at 14, Dennis Wheatley's *The Devil Rides Out* thrilled me. When the Duc de Richlieu was confronted by demons from the darkest pit he only had to call out 'Fundamenta eius in montibus sanctus!' and the foul creatures would shrivel into a chicken nuggets. I stored that one away in my memory banks in case I ever needed it. Fifty years later when I decided to translate it my reaction was the simple sonic: *Eh?* Those particular Words of Power, as I thought them, meant: 'His foundation in the sacred mountain'. I can't imagine that even the wimpiest fiend would take fright at that one.

Now I've no doubt if I *had* been assailed by demons from the Abyss in those early days, then 'Fundamenta eius in montibus sanctus!' would have blasted them back into their endless night. Not by the volume, certainly not by the meaning, but possibly by whatever inner intensity I could summon from within.

Of course if you've got any sort of soul within you (and I agree with Gurdjieff that not everyone has), then you will have experienced moments in the countryside, or even in your car, when you've felt compelled and inspired to chant or sing at the top of your voice. It might be some private mantra, some meaningful song or poetry that you just have to declaim. I still do that. Usually on remote beaches in West Wales. I'm compelled to recite Dylan Thomas' *Fern Hill* which, as far as I'm concerned, is the one of the greatest poems ever written, up there with Tennyson's Charge *of the Light Brigade,* or else the nonsensical *Jabberwocky* by Lewis Carroll.

In truth, in real magick, volume is never needed. If *All is One* and *One is All,* as Katharine might have overheard in Alexandria, then the Beings we seek to stir are all within us. Sometimes (and you will know when) you might want to voice your invocation more as a statement of intent – a way of pressing Enter – but you don't need to roar.

In one of his books William Gray talked about the 'wizards that peep and mutter'. That is, when they desperately needed to voice their invocations but equally desperately needed not to be heard by their neighbours, they would intone with their lips sealed. It would seem to any hostile people around that they they merely humming.

And often, in contrast, determined Silence will bring through the energies you seek to link with better than anything. The title 'I Am A Camera' springs to mind, though I'm not sure if Isherwood's actual book is relevant. There have been times when Margaret and I have stomped across landscapes chanting *Io Pan, Io Pan, Io Pan Pan* **Pan!** *just for the fun of it.* But most times, more usually, just walking silently in woodland with blank minds, walking za-zen, will do the trick.

I would add here that if anyone claims that they can keep their minds blank for long periods at a stretch then they're fibbing. As when you use the Celestial Gate technique you will always drift away, but simply bring the silence and blankness back again. Just look, like a camera, and say nowt.

So, in that Quiet Place in Wells Cathedral that is dedicated to St Katharine of Alexandria who seems to be a continuation of Minerva, did I then go on to ask her for anything?

Yes. And it's the all-important statement devised by Dion Fortune that members of her group had to express: 'I desire to Know in order to Serve'.

I am not, and never have been been a member of that society. And unless I can one day fathom the crucial text of the *Cosmic Doctrine* I'm not likely to become one in future. But I have an enormous respect and fondness for them and the real magick they work. And I truly believe that unless Magick is for the common good of the common person, there is no point in practising it.

Chapter 4

When you sit in silence long enough, you learn that silence has a motion. It glides over you without shape or form, exactly like water. Its color is silver. And silence has a sound you hear only after hours of wading inside it. The sound is soft, like flute notes rising up, like the words of glass speaking.

Anne Spollen *The Shape of Water*

Although other parts of the country are apparently being battered by Storm Freya we seem to be largely untouched. I'm having yet another of these damned fevers, which M feels is caused by Minerva trying to flush things out of me. I've drifted in an out of awakeness in the spare room, all night. The odd thing was, however, whenever I tried to sleep I found myself, in my fever, standing next to one of Margaret's friends from Brussels. No matter how often I drifted in and out of the mad quasi-sleep into semi-awakeness I still found myself next to her. There was nothing pervy going on. We were both fully clothed and not touching. No conversation, no emotional or intellectual exchanges. But she remained standing there. I asked Margaret if H was in any kind of trouble and was seeking help from her soul-group but no, she was – as far she knew – fine.

So because I'd been going to sleep every night visualising the Waters of the Gap I'm wondering if Sulis might be accessing my mind to try and create a mock-up of the sort we discussed earlier. You can do that in the rolling billows, apparently. When Bill Gray's father returned to him long after his death, Bill had no idea who this young man was. When I re-appear after my death I'm gonna be a real hunk.

These sort of images, in these circumstances, intrigue me. Many years ago a group photograph appeared of the girls who had attended Studley Park Agricultural College in 1921. The fella who showed me this was so excited because he recognised young Violet Mary Firth as being among them. I disagreed but he wouldn't have it. He just knew, knew to his bones that this was her. Since then the mite in question has been accepted without question as VMF and other people have insisted that, using this photograph, they have made a pertinent inner contact. I was pleased when Rebsie Fairholm did a brilliant and little-seen analysis of this in the magazine Lyra[viii] and

This is NOT VMF

agreed that this is probably not her. But at the end of the day if the spirit known as Dion Fortune wants to use this mask in order to make contact, then that's all that matters.

I've never tried to visualise Sulis herself but, if pressed, I'd have opted for matronly and dark-haired. Still, perhaps Sulis in this contact might *want* to be seen as a slim, blonde-haired Dane. Is this getting too bizarre? It's about to get worse…

In the last Sunday of January, before I began this book, we'd been to a course at the Equilibrium Centre in Corsham aimed at making contact with our Guides and learning about Quantum Healing. Margaret, given a quiet spot, has a clear sense of who her Guides are and how to contact and hear them. I, however, haven't a clue. This may seem odd, given that torrents of inner plane stuff have poured through me over many years, but They don't stay. Perhaps it's because I'm distrustful and don't have any written-in-concrete sense of what They are. Energies? Entities? When I've written up their stories they just seem to bugger off. Perhaps it's the same Energy/Entity assuming different forms – mock-ups – to use me for the next phase?

At times I've felt like a leaf in a current, and I know that other people in this magickal business have experienced the same. This is not me being self-pitying. On the contrary, although I've felt used and abused and enchanted and protected by their machinations I wouldn't change a bit of it. Well, except for that dreadful year of 73-

74 when I taught *real* demons at a school in Gloucester. I'll still never forgive one of them (who must be nearly 60 now) and hope that – inspired by Docimedis of the two-glove curse – he has lost his mind and eyes by this time. Not that the little git had much of a mind on his best day. I did used to 'peep and mutter' during those lessons just to get me through them. I'd get sacked for it these days.

However I do actually envy the many folk who can talk with loving confidence about their Guides. Sometimes, next to them, I feel like a Nobby No-Friends of the inner planes.

Before that course started a lady came in and took the last seat next to me. We talked, briefly, about what impulses had brought us here. 40-odd years ago I'd have asked her what Sign she was. These days I'm obsessed with the Spirit of Place and the energies beneath the Earth rather than the stars above. In fact, she confessed, since she had come to Bath she had started channelling Sulis!

I was excited but not surprised. Whenever any piece of Work begins, synchronistic meetings like this crop up all the time, many of them with no apparent meaning other than the inner contacts asking, perhaps: *Is **this** what you're looking for?*

Well, that's another side-story that may become relevant later because I haven't heard from her since. Because of my biographical interest in Aleister Crowley I imagine she suspects me of being a child-sacrificing Satanist. One day, if she ever asks, I'll point out that when Crowley boasted to the Daily Express in the 1900s, I think, about having regularly 'sacrificed babies' he was using the Oxbridge slang-term of that era for masturbation and was being entirely tongue-in-cheek. And all the editors and educated classes knew it and he didn't half sell a lot of papers for them when they branded him the Wickedest Man in the World. In truth, he was essentially a dreadful individual but no worse than many present-day rock stars.

However the main issue for me was at the end of the course when a lovely, fey, red-haired Wiccan woman told me that she saw Horus standing behind me. She knew nothing about me or my writing, but considering the amount of Work I've done over the years with the Egyptian pantheons I'd have been surprised if one of the *neters*, as they were called, did not appear somewhere. Though I would have expected it to be Anubis or (the much maligned and totally misunderstood) Set. Horus' appearance behind me was a surprise given that I was trying to attune to the Native Brit stuff. I brushed it aside.

The exasperating but often exhilarating part of working within any kind of Magickal Current is that you are often caught in swirlings within swirlings. It's never a straight flow. I couldn't see any kind of connection between Horus (and more about him in a moment) and Sulis. So I was somewhat startled when, after mentioning the notional title of this book in an email to Paul Dunne, he replied via his smart-phone, off the top of his head, on the way to work:

> A recent news eco story said a warm water storm is pouring through the oceans of the world right now - global sea warming. Thus Sulis energies are circling the globe right now. In the form of heated water streams. She is also the Goddess of the Sun, the Eye and Wells - the first two being Horus symbols. We are in the Age or Aeon of Horus now. Sulis a feminine aspect of Horus...... best PD.

I would never have guessed at that aspect of Horus in an aeon of Sundays. Being a semi-scholarly third-rate intellectual trying hard to be second-rate, that connection would *never* have come to me. In those terms, I still can't see it but maybe some of you can.

I'll tell you about Horus in a moment, but I should explain about PD, as he signed himself. I first became aware of him 20 odd years ago when a series of his essays appeared in various esoteric magazines. He seemed to be a cross between an *enfant terrible* and a *wunderkind*, made more palatable by the fact that when I met him he proved to be thoroughly engaging family man with a responsible job. I don't know anyone who knows as much about Magick as Paul. I wouldn't want to do a Vulcan Mind-meld with him because I'd end up like that woman in *Indiana Jones and the Crystal Skull* whose brain exploded from the ecstatick overload. Plus he's also got all the talents you'd expect a real magician to have. Of all the channellers I've known, I would trust his output beyond anyone. As for Horus....

Horus was one of the earliest Egyptian gods, and was the son of Isis and Osiris He was originally portrayed as a hawk or falcon and worshipped as a sun god and creator of the sky. His right eye represented the sun, and his left eye represented the moon.   I suspect that anyone reading this book will already have a pretty good take on what Horus  symbolised so I won't bang on too much. But stupidly, I suppose, despite all the work I've done about Horus over the years, and his famous Eye, until Paul mentioned it I never once connected the Eye of Sulis with the Eye of Horus.

I mentioned earlier that obscure little pamphlet in which Isis and Nephthys were seen to be powerful and hidden presences in my beloved Wiltshire. TBH (and note my masterful use of modern text-speak here) There's a part of me that thinks the author was clutching at straws. And yet, when I was contacting all the magicians and mysticks I knew for my book *Spirits of the Stones* and asked them what they *saw* at the ancient sites, many of them seemed to pick up influences of Egypt. The pamphlet is so odd that I've included it verbatim in the Appendix so readers can make their own decisions about it. It's a ridiculous, mad, unbalanced piece of work and I absolutely love it.

Of course it would be easy to create a story around Rendel Harris' thesis and make it all fit - which is what happens so often with hypnotic past-life regression. The 'storyline' here would be that people escaped from the tyranny of the pharaoh Akhnaton (who I see as a cross between David Koresh and L. Ron Hubbard). After long journeying westward they eventually settled down around Holt, Great Chalfield and Bath, thereby implanting their worship of Isis and Nephthys into the neurolithic pathways of the landscape. (That's a good word *neurolithic*: I coined it myself.) Of course, if Isis and Nephthys are here, then their children Horus and Anubis would not be far behind. Indeed Rendel Harris sees traces of the latter in the Dogwell in Holt (of which I've never heard and can't trace) and is sure that the word 'whippet' is a variant of W*epawet*, another name for Anubis. He also argues that Gypsy Lane in that same small village of Holt was originally 'gyptian Lane. There wasn't much mention of Horus in his thesis but if that Wiccan lady was right then he's been standing behind me all along.

But you have to understand how jaw-dropping Rendel's booklet is to Margaret and myself. Holt is a small and utterly unexceptional village about three miles from us. It is cut in two by a narrow but busy road, has a small village green, one garage, two nice pubs, one church of St Katherine and an excellent cafe. As far as I'm aware the only myth and legend attached to the place is that Diana Spencer lost her virginity to Prince Charles here when they stopped the royal train overnight in the Holt railway sidings. I don't know where these are, or if they even exist, and of course wouldn't know if there was even the merest tincture of truth in the tale, but the story persisted for a long time. *Holt...?!* said with astonishment. Imagine if a tiny township near you or even a local burger shop was suddenly invested with having been a refuge for, say, Atlantean colonists. You'd frown and say the only Word appropriate: *What??!!*

Now... while we're on the topic of Horus, for those who don't know...

According to Aleister Crowley (who died in 1947) the last three Aeons have been (1) the Aeon of Isis, (2) the Aeon of Osiris, and (3) the Aeon of Horus, which began in 1904. In an early essay about the latter he outlined some of what we might expect, initially, from the early years of the Horus, the Crowned and Conquering Child:

- The growth of innocence and irresponsibility.
- a childlike confidence in progress.
- The emergence of infantile cults like Communism, Fascism, Pacifism, Health Crazes, and Occultism.
- Religions becoming sentimentalised to the point of practical extinction.
- The popularity of methods for 'soothing fractious infants,' such as the cinema, football pools, and guessing competitions.
- Sport and 'the babyish enthusiasms and rages which it excites, whole nations disturbed by disputes between boys'.
- We are all treated as imbecile children - there is censorship and 'they won't trust us to cross the roads at will'.

He wasn't wrong, was he? He did conclude, however, that the Child Horus would eventually grow up.

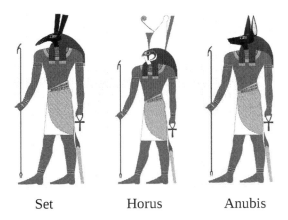

Set   Horus   Anubis

And while we're on the topic, I **don't** accept that this is the Age of Aquarius. We're not even in its dawning. For the past two thousand years, though, the sun has been located in front of the constellation Pisces at the time of the vernal equinox. That's the significance of the so-called Piscean Age. At some point, the sun at this equinox will be in front of Aquarius. *That's* when the Age of Aquarius begins. Most astronomers insist that this won't happen for a few more centuries yet. So we are still in the Age of Pisces, the Water Sign, if you use that system. Me, I'm quite happy to be a contrarian and accept that this is the Aeon of Horus.

So... what on earth is the hawk-headed Horus doing in our simple book about Wiltshire wells? To tell the truth I don't know and I'm rather troubled that this whole project has taken a somewhat Cosmick tone at the moment. I only want streams, wells, waters, ponds and picnics, preferably on sunny days and all within a few miles of where I live. Y'see I know that the Mystery Traditions of Egypt, Greece, Scandinavia, Persia, China, Maya and the rest all exist within us, layered like stratas of rock. You can access the innermost temples of Khem from your room on the tenth floor of a building in Kentucky (as I first did in Kirwan Tower Lexington many years ago), or from the Spring of the Green Man in Conkwell, in Wiltshire, when I wrote *Earth God Rising*. But at this moment I don't want to get drawn into these whorls and eddies, as I see them being. I've known too many people over the years getting swept along by their Quests before getting sucked into side currents that won't let them go.

I've been there, done that. And I think if anyone can throw me a line and save me here it's Julius Caesar...

When Caesar wrote what became known as *The Gallic Wars*, describing in the third person his experiences in Gaul between 58 and 52 BCE, he very much had an eye on his audience back home. That is to say his commentaries are forgivably biased and he was writing to enhance his reputation, passing blame for defeats, justifying his own actions, but probably giving an accurate report of the basic facts. When it came to describing the Druids and their deities he famously noted:

> Among the gods, they most worship Mercury. There are numerous images of him; they declare him the inventor of all arts, the guide for every road and journey, and they deem him to have the greatest influence for all money-making and traffic. After him they set Apollo, Mars, Jupiter, and Minerva. Of these deities they have almost the same idea as all other nations: Apollo drives away diseases, Minerva supplies the first principles of arts and crafts, Jupiter holds the empire of heaven, Mars controls wars.

Of course the Native Brits would have had no idea who Mercury was. Caesar was simply using Roman terms as approximations for non-Roman deities.

And I think that this is what Rendel Harris was doing, albeit unconsciously, when he had his blinding revelations about twin goddesses in Wiltshire. He would touch upon the inner energies first, and then other parts of his psyche would step in and find the nearest equivalent. Had he been a scholar of the Norse traditions, I've no doubt that his little booklet might have been called *Freya and Frigg in Wiltshire and Around.* (And oddly enough, given that we finally defeated the Great Heathen Army led by Guthrum the Dane at nearby Edington in 878 CE, there are enough examples of those two deities half-buried in the collective unconscious to make such a pamphlet tenable!)

So I think that this might sort out the confusion I feel around the whirlpool of Sulis. It might help me keep an eye upon her central energies and not get too distracted.

Plus I can also invoke that quote from Dion Fortune's wonderful novel *The Sea Priestess:* 'All gods are one God, and all goddesses are one Goddess, and there is one Initiator.' I don't know what she means by that last: *there is one Initiator...*But I totally get the first part. All is One. Or, as Arthur Guirdham noted in a different context elsewhere, *We are One Another.*

So, regardless of whether you give the god or goddess an Egyptian or Greek or Celtic name, it is the same energy. Likewise, depending on who makes contact with me as an individual for whatever reason, I may respond to: Dad, Alan, Al, Mr Richardson, Grandad, Walter Prince of Softies (in the eyes of my old pal Maxwell), or the occasional Bonny Lad, when I'm up North. There is one central essence to me, but I will respond to each name in differing ways.

Now I really want to get back toward Sulis herself, and enter that Gap from which her waters poured, and find other Gaps and Cracks and Eyes in my local landscape from which I can listen to her. And as I write this I'm struck by that simple phrase I used above: 'help me keep an eye on...'

We all do this from time to time: we keep an eye on our children, our bank accounts, the state of our tyres and so on *ad infinitum* as Caesar might say. I thought I'd dip into Phil Quinn's excellent *Holy Wells of Bath & Bristol Region.* In talking about Sulis at Bath he notes:

> A further examination of pagan Celtic mythology suggests that wells were seen as the 'eye' of an earth deity... This derivation... adds weight to the idea that springs and wells and holy wells in particular, could have been seen as places to commune, face to face, with supernatural beings. Further support occurs for this theory in Wales where the word *Llygad*, which means 'eye' is used to denote the source of a river or stream, an idea supported by Janet and Colin Bord in *Sacred Waters* who also note the saying 'you must not look in running water, because you look into God's eye'.[ix]

Now tomorrow, we really must get back on track with Sulis herself. Isis and Nepththys will have to take a back seat.

Chapter 5

They both listened silently to the water, which to them was not just water, but the voice of life, the voice of Being, the voice of perpetual Becoming.

Hermann Hesse, *Siddharta*

Last night I had a long dream about digging narrow, square channels under the earth, helped by a celebrity and a context so absurd that I hesitate to mention him. But I suppose I must – I'll dare to say it - why would Kevin Costner's Robin Hood be working underground with me? That aspect of it was pure absurdity and I'm only thankful it wasn't Simon Cowell. I knew it was ridiculous even as I was dreaming it. But then it segued into something more intense and every bit as lively and wakeful as the contact with the Fisher King...

Suddenly this small and **extremely** angry person burst into my awareness. He was half my height, *very* broad and muscular and bare chested. He had a pinched, pointy face, wore a brimmed hat and clutched a large hammer, I suppose it was, whose shaft was a long as himself. And my goodness he was angry!

I'm not sure if he was on the attack but suddenly he was pinned down by four other presences whom I couldn't identify because I was so busy concentrating on the little chap's exploding rage.

I won't hurt you, I reassured. *No-one will hurt you. Trust me I will never hurt you.*

In my mind I asked what I should call him. I instantly got the name *Joh* in return. Then it ended.

At that moment Margaret came into the room, saying somewhat anxiously that we had no water. Nothing was coming out of any taps. Still somewhat buzzing from this odd little person in my psyche, I found a small trickle came out of our cold tap that was only a little stronger than the flow at Cat's Well.

Is this enemy action, I thought? *Is the Fisher King getting his revenge?*

I'm still not apologising.

In the event everyone in the street had the same problem, caused by a burst pipe somewhere that required strong men in hard hats and orange high-viz jackets using big diggers to get down to the break.

Perhaps that dream of me being underground cutting channels meant that my unconscious had picked up this problem and relayed the information in its own way?

Later on, we wondered what this hammer-wielding being might have been, other than a fanciful, meaningless eruption from an intense dream-state. We were inclined to think that this might have been – I know this sounds preposterous – one of the trolls of Trowbridge, outraged by having his realm breached. This is not *so* unlikely: in Iceland even today, certain roads and building works have been abandoned because it was felt that elves, trolls and other hidden beings were being disturbed. We liked Iceland and heard enough up there to realise that even the most sober individual will accept this possibility. The Huldufolk (the hidden ones) are deeply ingrained in Icelandic society and these traditions are taken very seriously.

So I think *Joh* was a Trowbridge Troll. You see there is no agreed etymology for the name of this town, other than it *might* have been a half-hearted corruption of Tree Bridge - which I'm telling you all now is wrong. There is actually a Trowle Common at the edge of this small town - which takes us back into the realms of Norse mythology and Scandinavian folklore. In fact Wiltshire abounds with place names derived from Keltic, Roman, Saxon, Scandinavian and Danish elements.

Again, I'm getting side-tracked in our search for Sulis but I have to admit it's rather pleasant. And if the Waters of Sulis have come from the very depths of the Earth, then she would be totally aware of this small and very potent troll and may have sent him to say hello.

I'll let you know if *Joh* makes any other appearance in our lives as we work on this book but I rather think he'd be very happy to be left alone.

Margaret is off for a week's retreat to Cyprus tomorrow to recharge after some difficult months work-wise and health-wise last year. I've warned her to watch out for the half-faery Melusine of Lusignan, plus disenchanted Templar revenants when she's over there, both of which gave us some tricksy undercurrents of tension when we did *The Templar Door.* I'm not sure she listened.

But I'm feeling slightly guilty in that here, in the fifth chapter, I'm banging on about myself. I have not yet offered my dozen readers any techniques to experience the Magick of Water for themselves.

Meanwhile, until we can get back to trips and travels across Wiltshire and its wells again, consider these...

Everyone on this planet has experienced Sulis. Get into your Time Machine and visit the Sacred Springs of Aquae Sulis when the Romans first developed the buildings. Then, while remaining on the same spot, see the waters emerging from the earth during the Celtic period when you couldn't move for shaman-like druids and druidesses. And then go even further back, to squinny at the peoples whose origins we still don't really know and stand with them, putting your left hand into the water and feeling its uncanny warmth.

There will be a lot of women present because they, intimately and infinitely, will feel an immediate parallel between these warm, flowing waters coming from the Gap and their own waters after they broke, when giving birth. Everyone reading this will have some sense, sunk at unfathomable depths of the unconscious, of a time when they knew nothing except the sublime warmth of the amniotic fluid in which they once swam, and the months in which subtle nourishments entered their bodies from a source they could never see nor yet understand; of a time when – hopefully – they were totally loved and protected and probably wanted to stay curled into themselves forever. Every mother, feeling and sipping Sulis' waters tumbling out of the crack, would have known that this liquid was special, an exact echo of that which had poured from their own crack.

Today, those Waters of the Gap, to use R.J. Stewart's felicitous term, first fell as rain around 10,000 years ago and then sank to a depth of about 2km below the earth's surface. There it was heated by high temperature rocks to an estimated 69°C before rising back up through one of the three springs in the centre of the City, namely the very odd Cross Spring, the Hetling Spring and the King's Spring, which supplies the main Roman Baths.

If these waters had a memory, and if you could access it, then you would see the rain falling at the end of the last Ice Age. In what we now call Britain you would see the levels of the North Sea rising and drowning the land bridges which connected it to the Continent, especially that of the splendidly named Doggerland which stretched from Britain's east coast to the Netherlands. Some have argued, convincingly, that Doggerland was the real site of Atlantis[x]. It was certainly the richest hunting, fowling and fishing ground in Europe in the Mesolithic period, until a mega-tsunami known as the Storegga Slide drowned it.

But you don't need to make either physical or imaginal or astral visits to the Roman Baths to get some sense of Sulis. As Paul Dunne wrote to me:

> Today, we could say that there is a Shrine to Sulis in every home, albeit in the form of a bath tub or a power shower. In her most mundane aspect Sulis is the Goddess of the bath or bathing room, as well as all spas, wells and the water mains piping of every village, town and city. Today the vast network of water piping connects the bathrooms of every home. An aspect of Sulis is thus watery connections, bathing and cleanliness. To bathe or shower is an aspect of true civilisation. Bringing cleanliness, refreshment and helping to keep us free from unpleasant odours and disease. Sulis is thus also a Goddess of Purity, with bathing before robing also being important in some forms of Ritual and Ceremonial

Magic. We could also say that Sulis represents personal cleansing in a magical sense.

And he's right of course. You will all have water sources in your house/apartment/dwelling. I'm sure you've all done the thing where, when you have a shower, you visualise it as light pouring down and over and indeed through you, washing away more than just material grime. The simple act of washing your hands with intent can be used to remove all sorts of unwanted and unpleasant energies as Pontius Pilate could have told you.

I described earlier the simple technique of creating the Celestial Gate as given by Tom Kenyon, whereby the individual may encounter 'celestial beings who may grace you with their guidance and instruction', as he wrote. And, I suggested, using the image of Sulis' orifice (if I might call it that) you can form a useful equivalent.

But the all-important thing is **effort**. Above all, original, creative effort. Many years ago a magician I knew of real power but not much wisdom devised a technique that he was certain would enable EVERYONE (his block capitals) to illuminate themselves. He was convinced that, using his simple piece of visualisation, factory hands would become Masters of the Temple overnight. When this didn't happen, and none of the people he advised had *any* success, he asked me if I could fine-tune the technique. Of course I couldn't. All I could point out was that while this worked for him it was hardly likely to work for anyone else if they had no interest in it. He couldn't quite get that. He was still thinking in terms of Occult Science.

In this respect, path-workings that *I* devise work well enough for *me*. Well... usually, but not always. Other peoples' path-workings that I've gone on have just been a sequence of images that – to me - are little better than short-stories. (Margaret will disagree when she reads this, as she has had very deep experiences when involved in groups using these.) The point is, don't be awed or intimidated by what others do.

So on a different level and in differing ways, you can summon up another version of the Celestial Gateway using Google Earth. Try to visit Cat's Well for starters. It's tricky to find and you won't actually see much, but the effort makes the gap between yourself and Katharine (and hence Sulis-Minerva) a tiny bit smaller. Or you can descend like a god from outer space and find the entrance to the imposing Roman Baths in the City of Bath itself; then mosey along with your mouse to the nearby and mysterious Cross Bath where Sulis was also worshipped (and I suspect still is). During excavations there they found a skull right at the bottom. Even better, if you really want to squinny at Sulis in all her power and fury, then try zooming down to the geysers in Yellowstone National Park, or any of the unpronounceable ones in Iceland. And if you don't use a pc or have access to this programme then simply create a mock-up of a Temple in your mind's eye (which is probably linked to Sulis' Eye) and use it to visit the goddess that way. Do something inspired by and with the water sources in your own home. Find local springs or ponds and try to track the source of your local river, even if it's just on a map. (My local river is the Avon. It has disputed sources at some point beyond one of the Royal residences in the Cotswolds; it merges into the sea at industrial Avonmouth, which has been described as one of the most dreadful places on the British coastline. Once I've thought of a suitable metaphor for that journey I'll try to sell it to Margaret.) But when you do get to the source, however you do it, then in your imagination follow the waters down to the depths of the earth and the fires below. And if you see *Joh*, or one of his cousins en route, say hello for me.

It doesn't matter if you're half a world away from the places I write about here. Once you become aware of Sulis, she becomes aware of you and will keep her Eye on you.

But always remember that you should never expect instant results. Stuff that I did in my teens has sometimes taken decades to work through, and always when I've been old enough to realise why it was necessary to take so long.

I adore that old Rod Taylor movie *The Time Machine*. When it first came out in 1960 I thought that the female lead Yvette Mimieux was the most beautiful woman in the whole history of human evolution. But mainly I liked the fact that his time travelling device didn't move an inch, yet the world around him changed profoundly. They used the same technique (almost) in the more recent film *Lucy,* starring Scarlet Johannson, although she wasn't in the same league as Yvette. (Mind you Ms Johannson also appeared as Mary Boleyn in *The Other Boleyn Girl,* and filming took place in that Great Chalfield Manor so beloved of Rendel Harris; maybe she's touched with odd magicks after all.)

I suppose this is why the thought of Sulis' waters falling onto the earth 10,000 years ago quite moved me. I like the idea of drinking the waters and downloading a few aeons of history into my gut. But does water have memory? Does it have consciousness?

In 1988 a French immunologist named Jacques Benveniste sought to prove the effectiveness of homeopathic remedies. He and his team at the French National Institute of Health and Medical Research diluted a solution of human antibodies in water to such a degree that there was almost no possibility that a single molecule of the antibody remained in the water solution. Nevertheless the white blood cells responded to the solutions just as though they had encountered the original antibody. However the effect was reported only when the solution was shaken violently during dilution. Benveniste then famously commented: 'It's like agitating a car key in the river, going miles downstream, extracting a few drops of water, and then starting one's car with the water.' It was a journalist commenting on the study who coined the rather lovely concept of 'water memory'.

While Benveniste's study seemed to demonstrate a mechanism by which homeopathic remedies could operate, the mechanism defied conventional scientific understanding. In the event the whole process became something of a *cause célèbre* and Benveniste's experiments were subjected to as many tests by sceptical hard-core scientific individuals as those imposed on Uri Geller and Matthew Manning in a different context. They even brought in the seriously deceptive and slippery James Randi, the conjuror and manic debunker of what he saw as pseudo-science and outright deception. Much later, a team run by the United States Department of Defense concluded that several positive results were noted but only when a particular one of Benveniste's researchers was running the equipment. Benveniste admitted to having noticed this himself. He stated that '...certain individuals consistently get digital effects and other individuals get no effects or block those effects.'

I wouldn't begin to speculate on the science involved. I can only state that homeopathy worked brilliantly for one of my daughters when she was a baby, but not at all for me as an adult. Yet I feel deep down that water does have a memory. Perhaps this is something to do with even more advanced Quantum things – you know the sort... where a particle (whatever that might be) behaves differently depending on whether you are observing it or not. Okay I'll snatch something from Google here because I'm walking on quicksand:

> When a quantum 'observer' is watching, Quantum mechanics states that particles can also behave as waves.... In other words, when under observation, electrons are being 'forced' to behave like particles and not like waves. Thus the mere act of observation affects the experimental findings

But it's not just the 'memory' of water that intrigues me. Over the years there have been undercurrents of alternative technologies using water that have been suppressed by greedy industrialists. - legends of cars and generators that have run on water. Not to mention the work of Viktor Schauberger in the 1920s and '30s who seems to have discovered a free energy source by quietly observing water in its natural environment. By some accounts – I don't know how credible – Adolf Hitler had plans of using his 'Implosion Technology' to power the Third Reich, while the Americans after the war tried to get him to build the world's most powerful hydrogen bomb using what he knew about water. He insisted that water is the product of the subtle energies that brought the Earth into being and is itself a living substance. I can go along with that. There's an enormously expensive biography about Schauberger entitled *One-Eye – the rediscovery of aether*. I haven't read it, even though the blurb on Amazon insists it is 'A must-read for anyone interested in Free Energy and a new society.' I'm in favour of both, actually, but I fear that this might be another distraction. Given the title, perhaps Sulis of the Eye spoke to Schauberger in the depths of his Austrian forest.

At this moment Margaret will be on a beach near Paphos, where Aphrodite was supposedly born. Me, I'm scribbling in my notepad, sitting on a 'love seat' at the top of St Catherine's Hill in Frome, underneath the Valentine Lamp. This is the last surviving gas lamp in Somerset. Every year at 5.30 pm on February 14th, the lamp's renovator sets off a rocket, summoning lantern-goers to the site. At 6:00pm he starts the lighting ceremony, using the original lamp lighters' pole.

The lamp even has a renovated George V posting box attached – for your love letter or Valentine card. Fortunately, we use Skype.

It is grey and warm here, and utterly still. On the way up I saw a magazine in the window of a charity shop with relevant articles. One, issue 99 of *Caduceus*, goes into some depth (no pun intended) about the Water Memory Research Conference in which the Nobel Laureates Professor Brian Josephson and Professor Luc Montaigner give substantial support to the idea that water has some very unusual properties indeed.

Then there was Masaru Emoto who died in 2014 aged 71. Since 1999, he published several volumes of a work entitled *Messages from Water*, which contain photographs of ice crystals and their accompanying experiment. His photos are famous now and there are a million examples on the internet done by him and others inspired by his work. He seemed to prove that emotional 'energies' and 'vibrations' could change the physical structure of water, showing that the latter was indeed a blueprint for our reality.

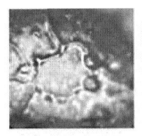 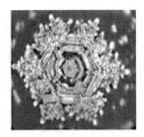

Water molecule before   Water molecule after
offering a prayer   offering a prayer

As you might expect, despite enormous popular appeal, it was branded as psuedo-science and James Randi was in there with the worst of Emoto's detractors. But there are levels in which he was completely wrong. Margaret and I often 'emoto' our own drinks just for the fun of it, and just in case. Though I wouldn't drink anything from Cat's Well no matter how much it had been emoto'd.

And *then*, along these same lines, is the wonderful story about Cleve Backstair who was formerly an interrogation specialist for the CIA. His Eureka Moment occurred one February morning in 1966 when he decided to monitor the Dracaena plant in his lab, utilizing polygraph equipment. He attached the electrodes to a leaf and began to think about ways that he might induce a surge in electrical activity in the plant. In humans, this surge in electrical activity is associated with intense emotions. He suddenly imagined burning the electroded leaf. The same instant this idea entered his mind, the polygraph pen shot to the top of the chart showing an extreme reaction on the part of the plant.

Amazed, he walked to his secretary's desk to retrieve a set of matches while pondering the possibility that this plant was somehow detecting the force of human intention. The plant reacted to the idea of being burnt.

When he returned with the matches, the plant was still showing the same high level reaction which would interfere with tracking additional changes on the chart. Backster decided to remove the threat by returning the matches to the desk.

At this point, the chart displayed a downward trend as the plant apparently began to calm down. When Backster attempted to repeat the same results by just *pretending* that he was going to burn the plant, there was no reaction. The plant seemed to sense the difference between real and artificial intent.

He eventually discovered that plants become attuned to their primary care takers, responding to both their positive and negative emotions and to their return after being away for a time. Chart findings also showed that plants prioritize the emotions of their primary care takers over the emotions of others nearby.

Personally I think that is wonderful. 40 years ago when Prince Charles confessed to talking to his plants, even the posh papers branded him a nutter. Now no-one bats an eyelid and we talk to our own plants as a matter of course. But if ever I learn that James Randi has been demolishing Backster's work as well then I'll make up a small lead sheet, curse him in reversed writing, mark it as *Deae Sulis Minerva*, submit it to the goddess somehow and hope the wretched little prestidigitator's balls drop off.

If he's got any.

I suppose the point I'm making is that as far as I'm concerned, it doesn't matter if Messrs. Benveniste, Schauberger, Emoto and Backster are sadly mistaken and drifting into the sneery, snotty waters that Randi and the like call psuedo-science. I remember Murry Hope, a true Deva, telling me how she believed that everything, no matter how small and apparently inanimate, had consciousness. When her old can-opener finally broke she buried it with loving thanks in the garden, so its constituents could decompose into the earth. Ridiculous, but so right. Thankfully we've got a big recycling centre in Trowbridge these days so I don't have to bury fridges or old microwaves in our garden. But I always thank them for their service when I drop them into the skip.

Likewise the characters I've just mentioned are, against all logic and likelihood, making intense and essentially loving connections with the elements. And you could assume that if plants did respond as Backster found, then it is because they were also well-watered.

Something that could equally apply to ourselves.

Chapter 6

Wishing is like water caught in a dam. You let a little trickle
of it escape and you don't think it's much, but in no time the
trickle has worn a channel and the edges fall in and the
water's doubled and then you get a flood carrying everything
away.

Winston Graham   *Marnie*

It's March 20th today. I'm not sure if Spring has quite sprung yet. I
suppose I should do something sacred but in fact I'm scribbling this
in the Field Kitchen cafe in Holt. It's very nice here, first thing. They
have long tables which remind me of things I might have
experienced in another life, in a monks' refectory.

According to the newspaper the cafe provided, within 25 years
England will face a 'jaws of death' situation in which there won't be
enough clean water because of the rising population and the ultimate
effects of climate change.

It also says that tomorrow night will be a super Worm Moon and
tells me when and where I should look out for it, adding that a Near-
Earth meteorite will also cross our skies at the same time. I'll keep
the bedroom curtains open again and hope to suck up things from its
light.

Must tell Margaret to look out for these in Cyprus…

Given that news about the water shortages, once I've finished my
breakfast I really must try and find the Dog Well that Rendel Harris
mentioned; and then go to St Katharine's Church which is tucked
away behind the village green.

Because I'm sitting in the far corner of the cafe and there's no-
one near, I'm doing the 'peeping and muttering' thing again, intoning
the name of Anubis (Anpu) to see if the Opener of the Way might get
energised and help me in finding this well or least cause a few mini-
marvels.

There are two very small lakes behind this cafe and a small and
apparently deep and dangerous Dawes Pond before it, but no sign of

any capped well, although water pours from the pond and joins a small but vigorous stream that runs through the village from north to south. I can't find a name for the stream. Would this be strong enough to power whatever engines they might have needed for the Woollen Industry that was such a feature of this area? I doubt it, but then what do I know about the Woollen Industry other than it was only made possible by flowing waters?

No sign of any capped well though. Margaret would probably have led me straight there, as she has an uncanny affinity for finding such lost things. I figured I'd be more likely to track it down at the library at nearby Bradford on Avon later. So I left my car at the cafe and made my way to St Katharine's Church.

Before I went there I'd tried to find out details about the place, but there were surprisingly few. One source suggested it was built as recently as 1891, although adding confusingly that it had 'early work in the south porch (c1300).' Even Nikolaus Pevsner could only offer that there was a niche above the west window with two wheels under it and wheels also in the battlements. In fact, as I found out much later it was known that a chapel existed  here in the early 12th century, as the Abbess of Shaftesbury gave it land. It was also mentioned in 1288-9 and it would seem that it was partially or substantially rebuilt in the 13th century, with a tower added in the 15th century. There is a very worn carving of a Green Man on the wall and also a dog-like beast with long ears trying to eat a serpent, so maybe Anubis was making an appearance after all.

 When I arrived, the outer door of the porch was open but, unusually for English churches even in this dreadful era, the inner door was locked. I'm sure that is symbolic, somehow. Perhaps there are mysteries within that I'm not yet ready to access.

The church itself gives ways to open fields and I remember many years ago standing at the farm gate and looking out across this vista, creating stories in my mind. You see I'd read somewhere that one of the fields across there was once known as Starveall. That is not an unusual name in this county, actually, and is usually an insulting term applied to farms that were badly managed. Yet I'd read something saying that *this* Starveall was actually a corruption of Star Fall. I had always wanted to see or touch a meteorite, and the thought of one falling to the earth here in late medieval times was quite exciting. I hope the one that flashes across our air-space tomorrow night lands in our garden. I won't tell a soul.

Looking at the map, it was somewhere in that region that the Holt railway sidings were – and perhaps still are – where His Royal Highness first gave young Diana a good seeing to.

It was only when I turned away from the gate and walked back past the church that I noticed what no-one had mentioned in any description of the place. *No-one.*

There above the door, set into the wall and about half life size, was a wonderful carving of St Katharine herself. The photo I took with my useless phone is not very good, but there are her wheels in the background. She looks at the sword she holds in her right hand (and Minerva had warlike aspects); I don't know what that feathery thing is she holds in her left. Her feet rest upon

those two spiky things that point downward. I first thought they were her legs.

I know that I'm guilty of a bit of pareidolia, here, which is the sort of word that James Randi might use to 'explain' things away. That is, the psychological phenomenon that causes people to see patterns and even faces in random stimuli. This is what enables them to see pyramids, faces, crashed spaceships and hot dog stalls in photographs of the Martian surface. But to me, looking at that lovely statue of Katharine, there is an inverted version the druidic Awen emerging from the modern light fitting.

A quick google describes this symbol as:

> ...the two outer rays representing male and female energy and the central ray the balance between them. It also represents the three domains of earth, sky and sea; mind, body and spirit. On the whole, Awen is considered a symbol of inspiration and divine illumination for poets, writers, artists and creatives.

Of course if I could get up there on a ladder, assuming the vicar wouldn't have me arrested, I'm sure I might find something far more mundane. But at the moment it doesn't matter. Katharine has been, in my local area, an almost forgotten figure and this wonderful representation has been effectively invisible to the various people who have commented on the church over the centuries. To me, this is an example of Katharine (and thus also Sulis-Minerva), being evoked to visible appearance and yet hiding in plain sight.

When Margaret gets back I'll take her to the Field Kitchen, treat her to a Full English Breakfast, and sashay along to the church with her to see if *she* can get us past that inner door.

Well, still somewhat thrumming from this find, I made my way back to my car, peeping and muttering through the dark underbelly of Holt itself, which I've never explored before. Of course, I say that tongue in cheek, as I don't think I passed a house that I wouldn't be happy to own. I felt that I really should walk across the fields to Great Chalfield seeing as I was so close. But it was a teensy bit muddy and I hate mud. Even with posh walking boots and all the geeky gear I try to avoid the stuff. I think I inherited this via the DNA of my grandfather, that modest and much-decorated war hero who fought throughout the Great War and lived to avoid telling the tale. Or maybe I'm just a delicate flower, more Oscar Wilde than Andy McNab.

So I drove, but as concession to all things healthy I put our little car into Eco Mode which meant it tootled through the very narrow lanes using 600cc of its potential. I know I know… Our daughters and their partners regard this vehicle with some scorn, as if it's something out of Toy-town, but I point out that it does about 8000 miles to the gallon, its 4×4 ability can outperform the legendary Land Rover Defender, and its road tax is only £30 a year, which is about one twentieth of what *they* have to pay for their gas guzzling monsters. Plus the grandchildren call this Granny and Grandad's Magick Car, so you can't get higher praise than that. And when you take it out of Eco Mode (as Margaret always does) it uses its full 870cc and accelerates like a stabbed rat.

I must say though, the peeping and muttering of Anpu didn't seem to evoke any appropriate omens or totems on this short journey: no black dogs, owls, hawks or serpents. I sat outside the truly magickal Great Chalfield with its moat and visualised the overshadowing image of Great Isis, but can't say that anything cosmick happened. Mind you, I realised later, that perhaps I should have been intoning *Heru* instead, if that deity really was lurking behind me as the Wiccan lady saw. I'll try that next time.

So then I went to the excellent library at Bradford on Avon, a small picture-book town where there are still Alms Houses dedicated to Katharine. When Margaret was young she worked as a lifeguard at the swimming pool. I, to my shame, cannot swim, and tell her that I'm congenitally unable to float; she pooh-poohs this. Perhaps, as part of my search within the Waters of the Gaps, I should put swimming lessons on my bucket list. Maybe I'll find Sulis this way.

To my surprise and delight I found out more than I expected about Holt and the fabled Dog Well. It is indeed capped off and hidden by modern buildings. But during the time it was in fashion in the early 1700s, Holt was regarded as an eminent little Spa Town, and something of a rival to the mighty Bath, some ten miles away.

Margaret's reaction when I texted her this was the same as mine:

Holt?

Holt??!!

It's rather like finding that the quiet little fella putting the bins out next door was once a member of the notorious and renegade Military Reaction Force in Northern Ireland at the height of the Troubles, and had been tasked to assassinate Martin McGuiness but got stood down at the last moment. (This is true, by the way.)

Or that the tiny, shrivelled woman I got library books for once commanded an Ack Ack battery during World War II and downed a couple of Heinkels. (This is true also.)

In fact Holt water from its well had the royal seal of approval and was sold in handsome bottles as far away as London, Southampton, Sarum, Reading, Worcester and Cambridge.

Collected and sold by one Henry Eyre whose motto for the Spa was *Veritas In Puteo* which means *Truth is in the Well*, they weren't modest in touting their water's powers. As Eyre wrote on the publicity:

> What has gained the Holt Waters such a Great Reputation is chiefly the wonderful Success they have had in all Scrofulous and Scorbutick cases, in the King's Evil, running Sores, inward Ulcers, incipient and even bleeding Cancers, inward and outward Piles; they immediately carry off any Breakings in the Face, Itching in the Skin, Giddiness in the Head; they have have done great Service in many Lethargick Cases and constantly give an Appetite. They are effectual in strengthening and healing Weaknesses in the Seminal Vessels, and are of Singular Benefit when drank after Mercurial prescriptions.

The reference to the benefits to be had after 'Mercurial prescriptions' is noteworthy. Mercury sulphate (a compound used as a red pigment in painting) was an essential part of treatment for sexual diseases such as gonorrhoea that were rampant in those years of unprotected and probably unprotectable sex.

Of course it easy to laugh at this and write Eyre off as little better than a Snake Oil salesman. But when I was researching in Bath's Central Library about the supposed benefits of 'taking the Waters', as they said, numerous modern physicians had insisted that the mineral-rich waters of Sulis had some profound and undeniable effects in treating certain conditions. In fact, at this very moment, the very old and prestigious Royal National Hospital for Rheumatic Diseases (known to all locals as 'The Min' - i.e. Mineral Water Hospital) still does advanced treatments using the waters of Aquae Sulis, and is set about a hundred yards from the Roman Baths themselves. Or as Jane Austen noted in *Emma*: 'Where the waters do agree, it is quite wonderful the relief they give.'

So what does this mean for our little Quest?

I suppose it means that the goddesses connected with the Sacred Waters all have a will to heal, and that we should call upon this aspect rather than hoping to blast someone, or else (as I often do) ask to win large sums of money on the Lotto. I think it was Masaru Emoto who quoted Dr. Fereydoon Batmanghelidj's words: 'It is chronic water shortage in the body that causes most diseases of the human body.' So what I vow to do now, and will get Margaret

79

involved, is when we 'Emoto' our glasses of water we will do so with the inner words: *To Sulis* and glug Her down. It won't do any harm, but I just wish I had one of those microscopes to see Before and After.

Which reminds me of something that keeps floating lightly into my mind…

At secondary school we had a Science teacher who told us solemnly that if you stood at the bottom of a well in broad daylight, then looked upward, you could see the stars. He explained the science behind this but I couldn't take it in as my friend Maxwell kept trying to jab me with a pair of dividers in revenge for some imagined slight. It turns out, however, that this is complete bollocks. Yet, as far as I'm concerned during our present search for the well-springs of Sulis, I'm continually being drawn to look upward, and often glimpse shining things within me that might be stars of a sort.

March 22nd this morning. I'd had a restless slumber and kept the curtains open but I didn't see the Worm Moon or the Near-Earth asteroid last night. Margaret, in Cyprus, didn't see then either and was kept awake by rowdy Russians who seem to be buying up most of the island, if the local papers there are right.

Sitting here in Trowbridge Library I've found out a little more about that carving on Katherine and no longer need to get a ladder and upset the vicar.

First, about the wheel…

When the Emperor Maxentius condemned Katherine to death because of her Christian views he brought up a spiked 'breaking wheel' to really inflict pain. At her touch, it shattered. Then he ordered her to be beheaded and she actually told him to commence. When her head was severed a milk-like substance rather than blood flowed from her neck. In her depictions she often carries a martyr's palm and the sword with which she was actually executed. And she is often depicted as having blonde, unbound hair (unbound as she is unmarried).

I also found, on-line, an excellent but copyrighted photograph of that carving, a wee snippet of which I'll dare to show here. Seen close up it is obvious that she sits above - not an inverted Awen - but the rim of her wheel...

Could the blonde figure that came to me during my fevered night actually have been Katharine rather than Sulis? Again, looking more into the background of the former, not a single authority has been able to make the case that she actually existed. It may well be that the Inner Plane Adeptii have used her to create the sort of 'mock-up' I mentioned earlier.

Just as I was finishing off that sentence our youngest daughter Lara Fay came in to do her own work for Uni. I told her about my recent findings and how, on the inner scheme of sacred and secret places, Holt was up there with Shambhala, Agartha, Cockaigne, Asgard, Rennes le Chateau and the Garden of Hesperides. She frowned and said:

Holt?
Holt??!!

At the moment, I think I've done all I can with the background of wells and spas and tutelary deities such as Minerva and Katherine, and can't wait until Margaret gets back and we can go out on our picnicks again.

Chapter 7

Have you also learned that secret from the river; that there is no such thing as time? That the river is everywhere at the same time, at the source and at the mouth, at the waterfall, at the ferry, at the current, in the ocean and in the mountains, everywhere and that the present only exists for it, not the shadow of the past nor the shadow of the future.

Hermann Hesse, *Siddhartha*

I was in the middle of one of my frequent Billy No-Mates dreams last night when M got back from Cyprus at almost exactly midnight, which is the traditional Witching Hour. Apart from the fact that she's home, and I'm utterly pleased to see her, she brought me a wonderful souvenir. It's easier to show this, actual size, than try to describe  the indescribable. Inside the globe is what seems to be a deformed creature of some sort. She tells me it's possibly a turtle but I'm going to do my pareidolia thing again and see it as Minerva's owl. When you shake it, snow swirls. She (Margaret, not Minerva) is the only person in the galaxy who has a deep understanding of the delight I take in such tat. In return I've told her she can borrow my fully illustrated *World Encyclopedia of Fighters & Bombers* and I'll even bookmark my favourites.[xi]

Now that she was home, I was determined to visit some local Bride Wells and Lady Wells set within a few miles of us and so very much within the influence of Sulis and her Gap, even though they are not hot and gushing. These lie below the scoured hillside-image of the Bratton White Horse that is the high point of what we regard, with harmless private conceit, as 'our kingdom'.

In fact there are numerous ancient places called Bridewell across the country but I found to my surprise that these are nearly all former prisons or 'houses of correction'. What happened was that Edward I, (1272-1307) gave a small palace to the City of London as a hospital, orphanage and prison. Because it was sited near an ancient holy well called St. Bride's (or St Bridget's) Well this became known as Bridewell. Later it was used mainly for the short-term confinement and punishment of petty offenders and anti-social misfits, such as

vagrants, itinerants, vagabonds and loose women. The name was passed on to the prison and this was later applied to the hundreds of others that were set up throughout the country on the same model. These Bridewells had a shocking reputation. In a biography of the prison reformer Elizabeth Fry, Mrs E R Pitman wrote, 'They made a point of visiting most of the jails and bridewells in the towns through which they passed, finding in some of them horrors far surpassing anything that Newgate could have shown them even in its unreformed days.'

The ones I wanted to visit were not in any way connected to anything punitive and this time I didn't get pixie-led as we followed the old dirt road past a golf course and a piggery (sacred animals, pigs!), and found the deep overgrown hollow that is the source of the Bridewell Springs. Margaret stayed halfway down the small hill, sitting down. I assumed she was giving me space to let me do my own inner thing; she didn't confess until we got home that she actually felt quite ill, and only came because she knew it was important to me.

Daft...

I have to say, despite the sacred names and the splendid vista of the overlooking White Horse, it was a sad place. I could almost imagine tumbleweed blowing down the dusty track. In the hollow was a brick construction up against the side of the rock, with a modern padlock on its sealed doors. Presumably in there are the emerging waters, like a bricked-up version of nearby Cat's Well. In fact, it struck me that this was almost a Bridewell of the punitive Victorian sort: used to keep offenders locked away. I felt there was some pretty deep symbolism involved here and a reflection of our times: the Waters of Bride actually barred from their natural flow.

Sorry I said to its waters, for the way we've neglected them.

If I'd been a bad lad I'd have gone down into the hollow and smashed the padlock off just to see what was inside. The more I thought about this place later that night, the more I felt that this hollow was once actually a pond. Apparently in Victorian times, before the present B3908 was built, they hefted water up onto the hill during dry times, so  there must have been a substantial volume here to make this possible. Today, coming out from under that brick structure, was only the teeniest and thinnest of rivulets that snaked its way past the piggery.

There is a definite, wearied atmosphere about this immediate expanse but no 'odour of sanctity' as D.H. Lawrence might have termed it. 150 million years ago this whole area was under a shallow sea and in 1994 the huge skeleton of a pliosaurus was unearthed near here by fossil hunter Simon Carpenter. The length of a bus, with sharp teeth the size of bananas, four huge flippers and crushingly powerful jaws, the pliosaur was the ultimate predator of the Jurassic seas that washed over here. It was eventually named as a *pliosaurus carpenteri* in honour of its finder, but to the locals it is called Doris. Standing atop the White Horse it is easy to imagine the seas below when Doris and her kind ruled them, when Ocean was the almighty power in this world – and still is. That was in the aeons before Sulis was even given a name.

It has been suggested that this little depressing hollow that was once at the bottom of the waves was in human times seen as a fertility spring, and Katy Jordan debates whether the name derives from the Anglo-Saxon 'bride' - a woman about to be married – or from St Bride or Brigid, the patron saint of midwives and newborn babies who derived in part from the Celtic triple goddess of similar name.[xii]

When I first started looking into the mysteries of Sulis it seemed that Brigid was a differing aspect, though as I ponder this I'm not sure if the flow is as direct as that between Sulis-Minerva and St. Katharine. To me, a trinity of Minerva/Brigit/Katharine doesn't quite gel, although most neo-Pagans accept the idea of the Triple Goddess with Maiden, Mother and Crone aspects. Brigid herself has a certain ambiguity in being at once a single goddess and also seen as three sisters, all named Brigid.

Minerva in contrast is part of a trinity that includes Diana and Vesta. Mind you, in looking at the qualities of Vesta, she is seen as the goddess of the hearth, home and family and her temple involved a sacred fire – all qualities attributed to Brigid. Diana, meanwhile, was goddess of the Moon, wild animals and nature, and we've already seen there was a prominent image of Luna within the Temple of Aquae Sulis.

I wish I could say that riding the water-flume of Sulis is taking me with great power and certainty toward the pool of her mysteries and that I will be able to make the Big Splash any moment now. But Brigid doesn't work for me, even though she is one of my favourite goddesses.

In the Egyptian traditions they tended to merge different deities through a process of syncretization, thereby, turning them into one single entity. Perhaps Sulis is doing the reverse: from a single spurt into my awareness she is splashing all over the place inside me, each droplet a different aspect of deity. From One into the All, I suppose.

I'm struggling here to collect the drops and gather them into a single vessel, but perhaps I should think in the following terms...

Vesta put on a new garb and became Brigid.

Minerva put on a new garb and became Katharine.

Perhaps I'm stuck in an eddy again or completely on the wrong tributary. If any reader can enlighten me, please do.

I should add that we first stumbled upon what may have been a Bride Well (or Brade Wyll) next to the church at Alton Priors in the east of the county when we were working on *The Templar Door.* Here there is a bubbling pond consisting of two spring-fed pools each flowing into separate springs which eventually converge. At different places, small bubbles break away from the bottom of the crystal clear water and perturb the surface. These are apparently caused by air being released from the local chalk aquifer up into the pools. The water here will eventually flow past the ancient sites of Marden, Durrington Walls and Stonehenge.

That Bride Well was, in its own quiet and modest way, spectacular. *This* one at the western end of the county, at the foot of the Salisbury Plain escarpment, was truly shabby in comparison.

I told Margaret about the local lore that when the clock on the church strikes midnight, the White Horse carven on the hill above would come down to drink here. It's a lovely image but it's a piece of local leg-pulling because the church doesn't have a clock.

I felt a bit guilty though, making a comparison with the burbling pond at Alton Priors. Here in our kingdom, this was a bit treacherous. So I just had to do an immediate re-visioning which went like this...

Despite its sad outer appearance I tried to see below the surface, tried to see that under our feet was a raging and enormously powerful torrent. And despite the shitty comparison with the outwardly magickal springs at Alton Priors there was no way that we were going to sneer – any more than we would sneer at a young girl with poor clothes. Truth is, I've met as many startling and sometimes soaring energies in cruddy backstreets as I have in sylvan glades. I've met ordinary people, written off as bimbos, Trowbridge Trouts and 'mere cleaners' who have had more magick and insight within them than the high-grade Adepts with their heads in Black Holes. There might not have been much flowing in this little place and making vortices and spiralling energies but it's OUR bridewell in OUR kingdom and we'll love it just as much.

Y'see I once wrote a tiny novella called *The Fat Git*, which a former girlfriend of mine from college days complained to me about, even though she never even opened the pages. She assumed I was being crass and size-ist. I can be hugely crass, but never size-ist. My paraphrase was that inside every Fat Git there's an Enchanter, wildly signalling to be seen: we have to contact that Enchanter somehow. One of the greatest souls I've ever met, now long dead, was a man with Downs Syndrome called Carlo, totally unprepossessing in every facial and bodily feature to the point of ugliness, yet he spoke to every woman of every shape, size, colour and age as if each one was the most wonderful and beautiful and interesting woman on the planet. He saw the Enchantresses in all of them. They adored him.

That paltry little flow in the ground below the White Horse was, therefore, the outward visible symbol of an inward, raging torrent of awesome beauty.

Alick Bartholomew, a writer on Water Mysteries, had his own epiphany in this respect. He had the realisation that he was embedded in water, and saw it as 'the infinite continuum of life in which all living creatures are contained.'

> I find being close to horses a bit scary. One day, the field where I walk regularly had three mares with their growing foals. I liked to take them apples as a treat, but when all six surrounded me, they felt a bit threatening. When I tried to visualise these lovely, powerful animals as part of my family through the water link, they seemed to become more like family and they were much less scary.

We are all One, because of water, he added, and suggested that it can even work with people.

Carlo certainly knew that.

Further along the road, just a couple of miles, is the Monkswell, also known as the Ladywell. This is largely unknown even to a great number of people in the village of Edington because it is completely unmarked. Despite having the Ordnance Survey co-ordinates I struggled to make sense of the map beforehand, found the on-line references ambiguous, and even tried to zoom down via Google Earth. It was only when daughter Jade treated me to tea at the delightful Pickleberry tea rooms and found a booklet called *The Footpaths of Edington* that I found crystal clear directions that would stop even me getting pixie-led.

It was probably constructed by the Bonshommes monks of Edington Priory to protect the spring which rises from the hillside and/or as a washhouse (lavatorium). The well house is built up against the small cliff from which the spring rises. It is a small but rather imposing building made from dressed stone with a pitched roof. The water issues from the rock in the corner of it and runs into a stone trough along one side. A metal pipe takes the water outside and is the source of the small stream that runs away from the well house. The spring, even during the hottest and driest of summers is never known to have failed.

Beside the stream a pump house drives water up to the top of the downs above the village for the use of grazing animals. For my American readers I would explain that in southern England the 'downs' are rounded and grass-covered hills that are typically composed of chalk. The name comes from the Old English dūn.

But I must confess now to being a bit of a phoney with all the information I've just given because we couldn't get anywhere near the place. This Ladywell is in an enclosed womb-shaped area surrounded by a jungle of trees and the backs of ancient houses. The *only* access is via a tiny right-of-way that comes down from the main road, the narrow, twisting, somewhat nasty B3908 of which I have many bad memories from when I had to drive along it in my very large Mobile Library. This road is used as a rat run by the many drivers wanting to avoid the carmageddon of traffic in Devizes. The nearest place we could park to get to the right-of-way was outside Edington Priory, and even a local lady whom we asked for directions or alternative ways into the womb urged us not to walk back along that road. From her expression I doubt if even she had visited the well herself although it must have been less than a hundred yards away.

The idea of a hidden, near inaccessible well is impossibly attractive to me, but although we drove around and around the area along its tiny back roads, swirling like the waters around a plug-hole, we could find no other way in, short of going through someone's back garden and perhaps assuming their identities while at it. Margaret made me promise not to try and walk back along that road when she wasn't around, as she knew I planned to do. Reluctantly, I promised, and I didn't keep my fingers crossed behind my back.

However, it was when we drove back to Edington Priory and pulled into their spacious car park that - perhaps - the real reason for our visit became evident.

A car pulled up next to us containing a charming young couple with clear trans-Atlantic accents. Whenever I hear such I always ask if they're from Canada. If they are, then they are pleased to be recognised as such. Canadians never like being mistaken for Americans. On the other hand, Americans I've met are always delighted to be mistaken for Canadians. I don't know why this is. For myself, my corrupted Northumbrian accent is is often mistaken for Irish. It doesn't bother me at all.

Gawd knows how this couple came to pass Edington Priory, as they were on their way from Stonehenge to Bath. Even a dodgy sat-nav would never have brought them this way. Nor were they visiting the Priory with touristy intent, as the fella was startled and charmed to find out that this very large and enigmatic building in the middle of nowhere was actually a *Church!* (his verbal italics), and that it was open and free of entry.

The rapport was instant and fun. If I hadn't been befuddled with our failed attempt to find the well I'd have taken them to tea at the nearby Edington Farm Shop. Instead I babbled. I gave them a mini-lecture about how it was here, after the battle of Ethandune, that England as a nation was formed. But I also enjoined them, with a dazzling, shining face no doubt, to visit the Roman Baths and the Temple of Sulis therein. I advised them also to get there early before being swamped by hordes of Chinese tourists. And before anyone tut-tuts, there is not a racist bone in my body and my lovely first ex-wife is Chinese.

They **promised** they would do this, **promised** they would go to see Sulis.

I didn't actually cry *Hi-Yo Silver!* as I rode off into their sunset but they must surely have thought: *Who **was** that man?* while checking wallet and pocketbook. I bet they thought I was an alien.

It was only last night, at the edge of sleep when I tried to revisit this area in vision, that I realised the true purpose of that particular pilgrimage: so that a young couple from Toronto might look upon the Waters of Sulis and soak up Her energies and learn... who knows what!?

The next Ladywell in Bradford on Avon was very easy to get to, even though it seems as though you're walking through peoples' back yards. This spring spurts from the hill above, on top of which is the rather lovely and quite holy Chapel of St Mary in which, during lost and lonely moments, I would visualise Isis and Osiris in the niches on either side of the altar. It seemed to work, somehow, and I don't think Mary minded. I could just as easily have used Jesus and Mary Magdalen or Horus and Hathor. I'd never thought of invoking Sulis in those days.

Even the locals get confused as to the whereabouts of the Ladywell and assume it is this one, in the area of Newtown, on the road toward Turleigh. In fact the true Ladywell is almost directly below this, but hidden away between the backs of the houses so that it looks like you're entering private property when actually it has ancient public access.

Depending on the weather, the water pours out from the true Ladywell in a torrent; there is a deep basin below in which you can see coins that people have thrown. In the top right hand corner there is a little blue plaque on the wall of the Mother and Child. In the top left corner there is notice from the council warning that because of landslips, the water is not fit to drink.

The stream itself flows away under the flagstones and there is a constant noise of flowing water here. Local gossip has it that despite the rather idyllic nature of this immediate area there is a very high rate of marital disasters and deep unhappiness.

The last time I visited was with third daughter Jade and Laura Jennings, magus of an American group using the full, heavy-duty Hermetic system of the Golden Dawn. Jade was then only two, a tiny golden-haired mite who is now, despite looking like a model, the first female fire fighter in West Wiltshire - literally the very incarnation of all the energies needed to channel water. Laura and I have had a healthy, loving antagonism for many years now (if she's still alive!) and on that occasion she dropped a coin into the waters and made her secret wish, ending with *So Mote it Be...*

Today, when Margaret and I tried to park in the centre of the small town, the whole place was heaving. Crowds of folk were coming out of the various churches. I assumed there must be some sort of town fete on, or a Pancake Race or maybe it was the annual Duck Race (don't ask!) but Margaret pointed that it was actually Good Friday and thus a Holy Day and holiday.

Being retired, I lose track of time and all the usual occasions that mark the year.

It was very hot, 26 degrees Centigrade, whereas in Crete (where some argue was the original Atlantis), it was only 11 degrees. I can't help feeling smug about that.

So we stood at the well in the shade between the houses and it really was lovely: ancient masonry, overhanging plants, the stream just visible beneath the flagstones as it rushes away down to the nearby River Avon. Margaret had to remove a ladybird from inside her sunglasses. No-one else was there.

I don't know what M asked for as she threw in her silver 20 pence piece to join a small collection of other coins. I did the same, visualsing what I wanted and ending with *So Mote it Be,* in memory of Laura. My wish was simple, and I can tell you now after the event. I wanted to win a sum of money – any sum – on the National Lotto scratch-card that I planned to buy immediately after this. Is that crass? I think of it more as a piece of research. As it happened, I won nothing. Perhaps I should have negotiated with the well-spirits and offered them a percentage of any winnings, somehow.

I still don't know if M's wish was granted.

I mentioned Alick Bartholew earlier and his sense that we are all One because of water. I found an article of his in *Nexus* when idly googling and burning through the midnight oils while Margaret was working in Brussels. Summarising the work done by Viktor Schauberger (whose name keeps cropping up everywhere), he argued that flowing water can be experienced in terms of *yin* and *yang*, and that the positive (*yang*) energies will generate in a natural river flowing sinuously across the landscape, recharging its energy towards the positive or *yang* on right-hand bend and towards the negative or *yin* on a left-hand bend. Schauberger noted that: 'This constant accumulation of y*in* and *yang* charges raises the energy level of the water so that it can perform its true role in nurturing the landscape. The same happens with our biological water.' Bartholomew goes on to say:

> The water molecule is made up of two small positively charged hydrogen atoms and one very large negatively charged oxygen atom; the strong bifurcated hydrogen bonds are unsymmetrical, which make water unstable and unpredictable. This instability belongs not only to the aquatic sphere; it is the guiding law of the Universe since its inception. Instability and unpredictability are the secret of matter's very existence, and the impulse for creativity... It is the restlessness of water that stimulates its pulsation and constant swinging between the *yin* and the *yang*.[xiii]

I'm not really up on Celtic equivalents of the *yins* and *yangs* of the universe so I have to use the mythological imagery which is best for me, and that brings me back to Horus again – or rather Horus conjoined with his brother-cousin (it's complicated!) Set.

The following image is an expression of the *yin-yang*: the balance of Darkness (Set) and Light (Horus). This is not really the place to go into any detail about the Set-Horus myths. Suffice to say, we make a mistake when we always associate Darkness with Evil and assume that Light is necessarily Good. After all, Torquemada and Himmler earnestly and passionately believed they were working with the Light. The Nazi magicians (and they did exist) believed that Dion Fortune's group and many others who were engaged in battles with them on the inner planes were all *Black* Magicians. So you can see it's never wise to be smug and write off people as being on the Dark Side simply because they challenge you.

Set himself has been the subject of one of the oldest and most on-going hatchet jobs of all time. Think of the *yin* as being his realm and you'll go some way to renewing him. It's one of the things I didn't like about Moyra Caldecott's mystical novels in that one character is invariably damned as evil and has to be defeated. Maybe that's why I was kept away from meeting her, as I'll explain later.

I don't doubt that pure evil exists, somehow, but it's not always in the obvious figures. Have *I* met evil? Perhaps. In my 20s, I worked in a large and now defunct home for children with learning disabilities in Combe Down, Bath. Although I had no managerial status and was simply a lowly nursing auxiliary, because I had the gift of the gab, I was usually trotted out to meet and greet visitors.

I sat in the office waiting to speak to the father of one of our children – let's call him Johnny – and the Home's infinitely placid and endlessly cuddly cat was dozing on the windowsill, in the light of the afternoon sun. The moment Johnny's dad entered the cat reared up, its tail vertical and rigid, its fur bristling and its claws came out. It actually hissed continually at the man as it backed out of the room and ran away.

Johnny's dad raised his eyebrows and shrugged. He proved to be entirely ordinary with a mild concern about his (very difficult) son. If I had not seen the cat's reaction I would not have seen anything remiss about him.

Then there was a morning in Glastonbury where I had attended a Shamanic journey run by Murry Hope. I was in company with Peter Larkworthy who was an influential but very discreet figure in the Wiccan tradition, and also Debbie Rice, who had been the Magus of the Fraternity of the Inner Light.

I can't remember where the journey went, but knowing Murry it was probably to do with Atlantis. Murry was then, to quote Raymond Chandler, 'A blonde to make a bishop kick a hole in a stained glass window'. She once told me that, although she was to marry five times, she never had much interest in what she called rumpy-pumpy. So when this 60 year old enchantress (who only looked about 30) put on her mask and went into role, a member of the group was so terrified he stumbled out white-faced, shivering and almost screaming.

Afterwards, Debbie ventured that the inner journey had been interesting; Peter felt that it was like the proverbial curate's egg – good in parts; as usual I could never follow the path-working and just waded around in the astral shallows.

We were joined in a cafe afterwards by a young professional couple who were both utterly beautiful and completely charming. Yet when they appeared I felt as if my solar plexus had been ripped open, my energies pouring out like the Water from the Gap. On a warm and sunny day I had to stop my teeth chattering and mentally visualised myself sealing up the huge tear while hoping that no-one would ask me any awkward questions as to why I was suddenly shrivelling into myself.

I remembered having read that similar had happened to Dr. Arthur Guirdham in connection with the presence of pure evil. Did the person who fled the shamanic journey feel something of this? Were the golden couple who joined us evil? I don't know. I doubt it. Neither Peter nor Debbie commented on them.

Perhaps I have had a similar effect on others at times without me knowing?

Last night I had a short but intense dream about Bladud, appearing in some temple-like place with an angry and aggressive attitude. This version of Bladud was heavily tattooed and bare chested but I didn't believe it was really Bladud coz he looked a lot like my old, oft-written-about pal Maxwell from my Ashington days. Mind you it couldn't have been an astral travelling Maxwell either, coz his Mam would have killed him if he'd ever got tattoos. In that tough mining community (both our fathers were coal-miners) it was the Mams who ruled. We all grew up with an intuitive knowledge of Great Mothers and Dark Goddesses because of them. And while I lay musing about this faux-Bladud I wondered what might have happened had Scargill won and saved the coal mines from closure during the 1970s. Simple. Miners would have had to be paid what they deserved, coz it was the worst job in the world and living within a tight, marvellous community was no compensation. So then, when they were paid properly and handsomely, they would naturally vote for a low-tax Conservative government rather than pay the 92% tax rate that the Labour governments imposed on all high earners in the 70s. I'd like to have seen Maxwell being sent to Eton. In fact he's really irritating me now because no matter how I type it, in whatever font, his name seems to be broken into two words: Max and Well.

So when I woke, unnerved by the Great Well's typically antic appearance, I planned to do some quick scribblings about the nature of the flying man Bladud rather than this tattooed imposter. But I was rather startled out of everything by my second meeting with an Alien.

Y'see I had been 'bothered' much of this morning and the previous night by the thought of Bladud and his connection with the Temple of Sulis and his attempt to fly. R.J. Stewart opined that this flight was part of an initiatic myth rather than an actual event by an actual person. Moyra Caldecott, who has often seemed to channel inner plane beings with provable accuracy, felt that he and his flight was actual.

If Bladud existed, and I like to think he did, he'd be no different to any boy I know who wondered if, by strapping something to their arms, they could leap from a wall and fly. I certainly tried that with predictable results. If I'd been a rich Prince of the Realm I'd have spent a large sum making proper hang-glider type wings. Perhaps it was because I was musing on the notion of flight that the next bizarre encounter happened.

 In *The Templar Door* I described how I had 'summoned up' such a being to visible appearance. This had been inspired by Timothy Good's book: *Earth – an Alien Enterprise* in which the author had sent out an almost whimsical telepathic challenge to any extra-terrestrials living incognito among us, to make contact with him in the Park-Sheraton Hotel, in central New York. To his surprise one did just that and passed various direct tests that he put to him telepathically before walking away. I liked the idea of that, so I sent out the same telepathic plea for similar. The next day, just outside Poundland in the shopping centre in Trowbridge, I was prodded very firmly in the back by a medium-sized fella, immaculately groomed, with silvery-blonde hair and piercing blue eyes who simply said a firm *Hello* then walked off. I was startled because *a*) I hadn't really expected any result to the inner broadcast and *b*) because the man looked like Ashtar, the existence/reality of whom I had long been dissing.

This morning, sitting in a cafe with the newspaper open, I again received a firm punch from behind on my shoulder and the same guy then faced me. He jabbed his finger on the photograph of Theresa May and her odious cabal of Remainers and said: 'That lot don't care what damage they do to humans,' and walked off.

Honestly, I don't really know what to make of both encounters. At all sounds ridiculous, I know. I'm far more inclined to believe in the historicity of Bladud than I am in the reality of Ashtar as an inner plane being. Maybe I'm missing a trick here, but I can only write up what I experienced.

If he appears again I'll put him in an arm-lock and demand to see his space-ship and how it works. It's the least I can do for the winged man known as Bladud.

Chapter 8

Water is the epitome of holism. It connects all of life; and life cannot exist without it. Spiritual and mystical experiences have a strong link with holism. Dynamic water, when it is alive and energised, performs the roles of initiating and operating all the processes of life. The most important function of biological water is to facilitate rapid inter-communication between cells and connective tissues, so that the organism can function as a coordinated whole.

Alick Bartholomew

An exasperating thing about my age (67½) is that I now have to refer to people that I knew, or wished I'd known, as 'the late....' I have a hard core list of the latter regrets that still make me wistful. To give you the short list: Although I corresponded with the Dark Lord himself, Kenneth Grant, I never met him. I wrote teenage fan letters to William Ernest Butler but I never met him either. In fact if family circumstances (i.e. my Mam threatening suicide) hadn't conspired against it, I would have gone to King Alfred's College in Winchester just to be near him. I think he would have become my teacher rather than William Gray over in Cheltenham. (Mind you, in the bizarre way that things have worked out, I do think that I accidentally tapped into a parallel life in which I *did* go to that college, as I described in an essay somewhere.[xiv]) And there is also Canon Anthony Duncan with whom I corresponded and spoke to on the phone but never met. And Arthur Guirdham of Cathar fame who lived across the fields from me. And – to get to the crux of the present book – Moyra Caldecott, whom I mentioned earlier.

Moyra died in Bath in 2015 at the age of 87. She was a prolific writer of highly regarded fiction, although I'd never read a single book of hers. I slap myself for that, too, considering that one of her trilogies about ancient Egypt, focusing on Akhenaten and Hatshepsut, resulted in Moyra being contacted by the pop star Tina

Turner, who paid for her to accompany her to Egypt, acting as a personal guide to the ancient sites. Indeed, the rumour went, Tina Turner felt that she was a reincarnation of Hatshepsut and you can see echoes of this in one of the Mad Max films. I corresponded with Moyra too, in the days when it was polite to include Stamped Addressed Envelopes (SAE's) in with your own letter. Of all the things I could have discussed I was solely concerned with babbling about a prominent hill near where she lived on the western edges of Bath known simply as Roundhill. It's modest enough as a simple hill and she had climbed it often, feeling a great magick there. But I had a bee in my bonnet about the place because on the old Victorian maps it is marked as High Barrow Hill and I was (and still am) certain it was a man made and Silbury-like construction - and why hadn't it been excavated?

So I never got to 'take off' with Moyra, so to speak, and was surprised to find she had written a novel about Bladud called *The Winged Man,* and had even founded the Bladud Society dedicated to raising awareness of Bath's Celtic heritage and, in her later years, performed her visionary poetry at local open mic events in the city. But I wasn't interested in Bladud then and was purely concerned with the sacred hills and barrows and standing stones. But also I have a marked degree of sociophobia which means that I can't spend too long in anyone's company without needing to escape. Honestly, it's a pain in the bum at times. Moyra was quite happy for me to pop around for tea and cakes but I chickened out. So, who knows, maybe one day I'll tap into a parallel life in which I *did* visit her, absorbed her idea that Roundhill was actually 'Sul's sacred hill' and picked up atmospheres of Bladud that might have enabled me to fly all those years ago.

I wrote in the opening pages of this book about what seemed to be an inner contact with Bladud. There is a statue of him in the Roman Baths which was probably made in the 1500s, painted, and makes him look like an old fart. The person who appeared behind me when I was having an angry communion with Pelles, the Fisher King, was young, athletic, with a wry, amused attitude and dressed in iridescent, kingfisher-type colours - which made me wonder if he had come to replace that older man who was forever rattling around at the edges of his Wasteland. But if you want to know why I've no time for the Holy Grail then you might want to see another essay I did in my book *Short Circuits – Essays in Otherness.* Actually, I think I'll include that in the Appendices too, because some are so awed by the Grail they can't see around it or feel its plastic edges.

As ever, I tend to assume that everyone will know about Bladud, but as I've always made that mistake it's not an age thing. Here is the outer stuff that you need to know...

The Welsh form of his name is *Blaiddyd*, meaning Wolf Lord, and in those days everyone in that area would be what we now think of as Welsh. His name was probably spelled with the (now obsolete) letter ð which was pronounced with a *th* sound, as in *th*ick. In later centuries this became rendered in print as a simple *d*. So, for example, the local site of Edington, which we will visit later, was once pronounced as *Eth*andune. His own name was probably pronounced as something like *Vla-thuth*, and R.J. Stewart  argues convincingly after looking at various Welsh, Gaelic and Gaulish roots that name can mean 'bright god', 'bright priest' or even 'bright dark', the latter being a 'typical example of Celtic duality in concept, and would again fit Bladud's career of glory and then ignominy.'[xv] He also points out that the elements of the King's name include Bal or Bel and then Dud or Dydd: 'He is therefore a priest of Bel, for the name is derived from Bel and Derwydd (the sun god and the druid). Baldud or Bladud or Blaidydd is the burning sun face of the temple pediment...'

He was sent by his father to be educated in Athens. Accounts vary as to when this was, ranging between 500, 740 or 863 BCE. The spread is so great that either he was a total myth, or the title Wolf Lord was a hereditary title, like that of Pendragon. Using one time-line, then upon his return to Britain he founded a university at Stamford in Lincolnshire, which flourished until it was suppressed by Saint Augustine of Canterbury (who died in 604 CE) on account of heresies which were taught there.

An intriguing aspect to his story is that while he was in Athens he actually contracted leprosy, so when he returned to this country he was imprisoned. The legend adds that before he managed to escape his mother gave him a golden ring, both as a keepsake and as a means to identify himself should there become a need. Once free he went into hiding and worked as a lowly swineherd at Swainswick on the eastern fringes of Bath, presumably at the foot of Solsbury Hill – yes, the same hill Peter Gabriel wrote his hit-song about and that we plan to visit when it's appropriate.

With pigs as his only company he took to watching them closely and after a while he noticed they were also beginning to be afflicted by his skin condition. Fearing the worst and to prevent his employer from finding out, he drove the pigs across a river. There he noticed the pigs were attracted to a boggy area of ground, wallowing in the warm mud from the hot water springs. According to the legend when the pigs came out of bog he scraped them clean and discovered their skin condition was cured.

With nothing to lose, Bladud decided to try the warm mud himself and to his astonishment he found that this also cured his skin condition.

Bladud returned to court where he was quickly identified by the gold ring his mother had given him. When he later became king he built Kaerbadum or Caervaddon (Bath), creating the hot springs there 'by the use of magic', and dedicated the city to the goddess Athena or Minerva.

The final part of his tale has him indulging in necromancy and, using information given by spirits of the dead, he rivalled Daedalus by constructing wings for himself. When he tried to fly from the Temple of Apollo he crashed and broke his neck and was succeeded by his son Leir – Shakespeare's King Lear.

There is a modern statue of him in the Parade Gardens next to the river. Apparently Bath City Council, acting mysteriously, kept it stored away for years until someone must have persuaded them that there are worse icons in this world. I can't make out what he's holding in his left hand. It looks likes an asthma inhaler, but I guess it isn't. I know a number of magicians (all of them female, actually) who have been able to imbue statues such as this with energies that make them more than mere lumps of stone. I don't know if  any of them have, or will in future, do this to our lad here. But it's certainly a huge improvement on the old clown that has overlooked the King Bath for the past few centuries.

In John Clark's *Bladud of Bath: The Archaeology of a Legend*, he argues that the bits about leprosy and the pigs were added to the story centuries later, and that the 'real' person was probably Prince Bleiddudd, Lord of Dyfed, described as generous and welcoming to artists, who once wrote a 9th-century Welsh poem called 'In Praise of Tenby'.

I like that idea. Tenby is our favourite sea-side town in Britain. Actually, make that in the whole of the spiral arm of our galaxy...

So that's the essentials of the Bladud myth. Whether there is any historical 'reality' behind this story is completely unimportant. For example, I don't have any hard and fast belief in Atlantis and where it was, whether this was Doggerland, Crete, around the Azores, somewhere in the Caribbean or even, because of a crustal slip of the Earth, now beneath the ice of Antarctica. William Gray suggested to me that it might not even have been on this planet at all and hinted that Mars was a likely contender. But I do believe that there is a level of consciousness and a dimension in which 'Atlantis' is fully explorable and packed with energies. The same goes for the likes of individuals such as King Arthur in his Camelot, Robin Hood in his Wildwood and also Bladud and his (very sacred) pigs.

To paraphrase Dion Fortune's Masters' comment:

> What Bladud is we cannot realise and it is a waste of time to try to do so, but we can imagine him on the astral plane and he can contact you through your imagination, and although your mental picture is not real or actual, the results of it are real and actual.

R.J. (Bob) Stewart's speculation that the name Bladud might mean 'bright dark' being an example of Celtic duality, is an important insight for me personally.

Some years ago I wrote a black-comic novel set in the present day based upon my adventures managing a specialist mobile library that took books to the elderly in remote parts of Wiltshire. For some reason I *had* to call it *Dark Light – a Neo-Templar Time Storm*. Margaret hated the title then and still does, but I *had* to use it. In fact I knew so little about the Templars at that time that I had no idea about the Beausant, their black and white battle flag, or their sometimes Manichean take on the universe.

So if anyone was going to be a Priest of Sulis' Mysteries, understanding the *yin* and *yang* of Her watery energies, then the bright-dark nature of Bladud is just what you need.

I think we've just about finished with the **All You Ever Wanted to Know About Bladud** section except to mention Abaris.

In Greek mythology Abaris the Hyperborean was a legendary sage and healer in his primary guise as Priest of Apollo. Just as modern folk in the West drool over the notion of Merlin and seek to make some sort of contact on varying levels, the Ancient Greeks felt the same about Abaris, as did the Ancientnt Egyptians with their master magician Kha'm-uas.

Abaris' homeland of Hyperborea was, according to Herodotus, blessed with eternal spring, resulting in a double harvest of grain per year, with most of the countryside covered in forests called the Garden of Apollo. According to Greek legend, the land of Hyperborea is a place of total perfection, with sunlight 24 hours a day.

When plague struck however, Abaris fled to Greece where he impressed everyone with his gifts of prophecy allied with a natural simplicity and honesty.

His legend grew. He was said to have travelled around the world, eating no food, with an arrow on which he could also fly. Plato classed him among the Thracian healers who, using incantations, worked upon the soul as well as the body. He was also credited with founding a temple to Persephone at Sparta and was seen as a cross between a shamanistic missionary and saviour-figure.

Of course, taking all these into account, the almost-as-legendary but very real personage of John Wood the Elder (1704-54), just knew beyond doubt that Hyperborea was actually in Britain and that Abaris was really Bladud. You can see the similarities.

It would be tempting to go into more detail about John Wood senior but I'd create a whirlpool from which I might find it hard to escape. Suffice to say that he surveyed Stonehenge and the Stanton Drew stone circles when no-one else had the slightest interest, was possibly involved in the early days of Freemasonry, created those buildings in Bath that made it what it is today, wrote extensively about sacred geometry, and argued that the myths of the supposed founder of Bath, King Bladud, were based on truth. He even added a bit more truth of his own. According to him, when Bladud returned to Britain 483BCE after his miracle workings in Greece he built:

- The city of Caerbrent, otherwise known as Caer Ennaint (the City of Ointment),
- Caer Yrn Naint Twymin (the City of the Warm Vale),
- Caer Palladur (the City of Pallas's Water),
- Troy Novant (the Turning Valley),
- Caer Badon (the City of the Bath),
- Hatbathan (the Hot Baths) or Ackmanchester (the place of the Oak Men).

That last was a reference to the Druids, for which group Bladud founded a University at nearby Stanton Drew whose standing stones Wood regarded as a model of the solar system. I've no idea where he got all that from but it's all magickal to my way of thinking.

People sometimes go a bit gooey when Freemasons are mentioned, as if they still wield awesome power and have cosmic insight into the real workings of the world. In the 19th and 20th Centuries if a man wanted to 'get on' then membership of a Lodge was almost compulsory. No matter that not one Mason in a thousand would have the slightest insight into what their rituals meant. I'm a great fan of the books by Christopher Knight and Robert Lomas who are themselves very high grade Masons and have done original research into the true origins of the Craft and the meaning of its ceremonies and grades. Knight commented once that when quizzing Brothers ranked above him about certain aspects, they just didn't have a clue.

I'm fascinated by Freemasonry and its true origins but have never been tempted to join unless I could go straight in at the 32nd Degree of the Scottish Rite without any fannying about in the lower ranks. Besides, the world has turned, and if a man wants to 'get on' these days then he really has to join a golf club.

And I would never *ever* do that...

I've been hoping that with all my inner work and the nightly use of the Celestial Gateway, that I might have had more appearances by Bladud or the delicious figure of Abaris the Hyperborean. And especially, Sulis coming to me in vision in the modern style of our Danish friend H. But while things have bubbled and flowed along and I have a continual sense of inner engagement with... *Something...* nothing spectacular has happened. Perhaps I am trying too hard, or shouting too loudly. Perhaps I should keep an Eye out for little things.

Not too long ago on a beach in Wales - Caswell Bay to exact – I thought I would try and summon up the wraith of Dylan Thomas. I didn't expect to 'see' him psychically, but I just wanted some kind of omen, or sending, like the auto-acknowledgement function you can get on emails. I'd seen a photo of Thomas at Caswell Bay when he was a young man, and as I can recite large chunks of his poems off by heart, I felt I was in with a chance. But... nothing.

Later on, at the very liminal sands of Whiteford Burrows further up the coast, I thought I'd try Ted Hughes. Now I have a great fascination for Hughes, who had a truly magickal background that few have acknowledged because of his understandable secrecy over his tragic private life. Even though he was Poet Laureate and had written oceans of poetry I could not quote a single line of his – and I don't know anyone who can. Yet he sometimes perks up in my mind as a flickering, priestly, magickal presence perhaps from the land of Khem. That time at the deserted Burrows (deserted because they're remote and most people don't get further than Rhossili Bay) I asked him just to send us a little symbol, a teensy-tiny sign. The tide was low and we were on the cusp of sea and estuary and the sun was high and the air was full ozone... It was all propitious as far as the

Elements went. Then Margaret picked up a shell, inside which was the very unusual sigil that I like to think was Hughes' gift to us both. I suppose it might also be a means of contact with some sort of Hughes-ian Muse.

I suppose what I'm trying to speculate is that in this odd business of Magick we use such images and ideas when they come floating in to us. John Wood the Elder made use of Bladud by linking him with the powerful myth of Abaris the Hyperborean, creating a kind of conduit for inspiration to flow. Now, sitting here brooding about it, I'm also going to link Ted Hughes with Abaris the Hyperborean.

I'll let you know how I get on.

Chapter 9

Death is water's close companion, and neither of them can be separated from us, for we are made of the versatilitiy of water and the closeness of death. Water doesn't belong to us, be we belong to water: when it has passed through our fingers and pores and bodies, nothing separates us from earth.

Emmi Itäranta, *Memory of Water*

The magnificent image that appears atop the pediment in the Roman Baths was once described as that of a Gorgon. Perhaps when it was all muddy and its curves and lines confused it might have seemed that way, but once it was cleaned up no-one could really continue to argue for this identity. If Sulis needed a consort or a priest then she couldn't have picked a finer fella than this one:

The question remains, who is it? Some writers have argued that Sul was actually a male and that this is him. Others feel, intuitively, that this was the god who greeted visitors to the Temple and led the way to the goddess, Sulis, in the dark and watery interior. Others still are certain that this is Bladud, as glimpsed by his wings, and that the snakes are a tribute to the healing powers of Aesculapius whom Bladud would have known about during his time in Greece.

But because of oceanic symbolism lower down on the pediment, the case has also been argued that this might be a sea god such as Neptune or Oceanus. His hair and beard do flow a bit like waves, and as the Temple of Sulis is a place of water and sea-gods are depicted with beards it is possible that is another syncretic aspect. Paul Dunne immediately felt that this was Pontus, the son of Aether and Gaia and primordial god (*protogenos*) of the sea. He was the sea itself, not merely its resident deity, who was born from earth at the dawn of creation.

Personally, I'm half-inclined to think this might instead be the almost unknown (in this country at least) deity Fontus, a *very* worn image of whom appears below.

Fontus, from 'Font' or 'Source' was a god of wells and springs – specifically a god of pure water. I've never had much interest in the basic Roman pantheons but I think there was/is a part of me that was connected with the Mithraic Mysteries. Not in any high level, but more as a clerk who got stabbed by a very wild Maxwell along Hadrian's Wall. The following from Wikipedia says an awful lot about Fontus that is relevant:

> Water as a source of regeneration played a role in the Mithraic mysteries, and inscriptions to *Fons Perennis* ('Eternal Spring' or 'Never-Failing Stream') have been found in mithraea. In one of the scenes of the Mithraic cycle, the god strikes a rock, which then gushes water. A Mithraic text explains that the stream was a source of life-giving water and immortal refreshment. Dedications to 'inanimate entities' from Mithraic narrative ritual, such as *Fons Perennis* and *Petra Genetrix* ('Generative Rock'), treat them as divine and capable of hearing, like the nymphs and healing powers to whom these are more often made.

That describes Aquae Sulis to a 'T'. Yet despite that, and however, tempting and tantalising all the other options may be, I would put my money on it being the face of Bel. Most people these days are happy to accept that this is an image of that Celtic sun-god and the more I research the more I'm inclined to agree.

Belenus/Belenos/Belinus/Bel/Beli Mawr are different names for the same deity from Celtic mythology. Intriguingly, Bel was also in the 3rd century, the patron deity of the Italian city of Aquilea. Known as the 'Fair Shining One', or 'The Shining God', he was one of the most ancient and widely worshipped Celtic deities and is associated with the ancient fire festival that is known today as Beltaine on May 1st. He was also associated with the horse and the wheel. Perhaps like Apollo, with whom he was identified in Caesar's mind, Belenos was thought to ride the sun across the sky in a horse-drawn chariot.

Bernhard Maier felt that the name may be from a Proto-Celtic *Guelenos,* containing a root for 'source or well', suggesting identification as a god of healing springs. *Bele*nos is the husband of Danu who is the mother of the gods of the Tuatha De Danann, gods of the Celts.

Miranda Green writing in her *Dictionary of Celtic Myth and Legend* noted:

> An epithet of Belenus may have been *Vindonnus.* Apollo Vindonnus had a temple at Essarois near Châtillon-sur-Seine in Burgundy. The sanctuary was based on a curative spring. Part of the temple pediment survives, bearing an inscription to the god and to the spirit of the springs and, above it, the head of a radiate sun-deity. Many votive objects were brought to the shrine, some of oak, and some of stone. Some offerings take the form of images of hands holding fruit or a cake; others represent the parts of the body requiring a cure. In many cases the pilgrims appear to have suffered from eye afflictions.

Although I will think of this being/energy/entity from now on as Bel, the multitude of names takes us back again to that quote in *The Sea Priestess:* 'All gods are one God, and all goddesses are one Goddess, and there is one Initiator.' I *still* don't understand the 'one Initiator' bit unless – just thinking about it now – it's *me.* If *All is One* and therefore *One is All,* then perhaps *I* am Bel, Fontus, Sul, Katharine and all the others. Just as, on another level, I am also Dad, Alan, Al, Mr Richardson, Grandad, and – I almost forgot – Jackanory, as the pupils nicknamed me when I taught in a London school. Can't think why.

Off to bed now. I'll have a good think about that last bit.

I did have a big argument over Bel at one time in the 1980s. This happened when I peeked over the walls of Belcombe Court on the edge of Bradford on Avon. It was privately owned then by a Mrs Woodroffe, and opened once a year through the National Gardens scheme. It has – or perhaps had – various follies in the grounds, a hint of a stone circle as I recall, and a very potent 'tump' or bell barrow in the very top of the grounds from which a serpent energy poured out once when I was in the bath at Murhill and trying to 'remote view' it. In a little leaflet that was floating around for the National Gardens thingy, it mentioned that the name was from the word Baal.

I was on tippy-toes and peering over with Simon Buxton, who was even then preparing to do that largely fictional book of his *The Shamanic Way of the Bee.* Mrs Woodroffe herself appeared on the other side of the wall and was – understandably - quite annoyed at this intrusion.

I said:

This is not really Baal's combe but Bel's combe.

She said:

It's Baal, of course it's Baal.

So I did what anyone would have done in such circumstances when faced with a tetchy woman who clearly had never heard of the ancient British sun-god... I invoked Robert Graves and *The White Goddess.* In that he noted how a number of places associated with Danes in this country are actually harking back much further to the children of Danu or Dôn. Thus, in the village of Winsley just a mile across the fields, as several places with names such as Dane Rise or Danes Bottom and the like. Might these, put together, refer to the husband and wife deities known as Bel and Dôn, I asked her?

She looked a bit glassy-eyed and so I left, but sent her a letter shortly after going into some detail about my arguments. The next year, in the leaflets about Belcombe, there was no mention of Baal. Actually she also invited me for tea when she received my letter but yet again I went shy.

But you know, forgetting about Bel for a moment, what I really wanted to ask this woman was: 'Are you perhaps the daughter or grand-daughter of Sir John Woodroffe? That is, Did one of your forebears write under the name of Arthur Avalon and publish in 1919 (utterly shocking for its time) *The Serpent Power – The Secrets of*

Tantric and Shaktic Yoga? Was your grandad a Master of Sex Magick?'

Some things are best left unasked.

I slept badly last night. I was awake at 3 am brooding about that image of Bel and felt compelled to go downstairs and work on it, using the simple free programme of Paint.Net. I reversed the colours, highlighted it, added effects and changed colours but then finally decided that what it *really* needed was a real pair of eyes. Hence the versions you will see in places throughout this text.

Mind you, I was pressured to use my *own* eyes and took clumsy photos using the camera on my laptop. I'm glad Margaret didn't come down and catch me at it as I must have looked a right eejit. Thankfully a still, small voice within told me **not** to sail down that stream of consciousness. While it might boost my already monstrous ego to see myself looking out of my own pages, it might be a bit too eldritch even by my standards. So I found a nice green orb on the internet, cloned it, and fitted them both onto the face of Bel in the design I hope to use for a cover. I do believe Bel was pleased with this. At last, he can actually see for himself where his consort Sulis might be flowing.

But for some reason or non-reason I was also reminded of the ritual mask found in the Roman Baths themselves which I had more or less ignored until now. This so clearly has echoes of the shamanic stuff that was almost universal in the ancient of days, even in earliest days of Egypt. (The Jobbing Wizard of deepest Wales, Mike Harris, spits feathers whenever anyone mentions the word 'shaman', as William G. Gray used to do with the word 'witch'. I must send him some eye-opening and very  scholarly links about Shamanism and Pre-Dynastic Egypt some day. *Shaman Shaman Shaman,* Mike, if you're ever reading this.)

I thought back to that simple shamanic journey I undertook with Murry Hope that day, but her mask was considerably more elegant than this fella's.

I've no idea where this is all flowing toward, incidentally...

Although the overall image of Bel with his locks, wings and serpents can be visually intense, the one thing that has always taken precedence for me is that marking on his brow. I like it when magicians and seers have seen markings in my own aura, just as much as when witches have seen Horus standing behind me or mediums have seen my Dad and even the somewhat legendary Moon Priest once known as Colonel Seymour. Dolores Ashcroft saw a marking on my brow which I took to be that of the Mithraic grade of Corvus. As I recounted in *The Templar Door,* the supra-ordinarily talented Dee Banton saw a glyph in my aura which foresaw that project a year before I even thought of it. William Gray saw bugger-all in my aura but probably wouldn't have told me even if he did.

So when I stumbled on that simple exercise of the Celestial Gateway I saw it as a means of doing Work in that precise area. And now, with Bel's green eyes upon me, I'm constantly drawn to that glyph on his brow...

What is that? And please don't say it's the Holy Dove descending! If the artist had sought to create a furrowed brow, it would not have looked like that. He would not have wanted just to fill space; the original carving is very large and he wouldn't have risked getting it wrong and having to start again. This is a specific marking on Bel's brow that would pass on information to anyone who saw it. Could it symbolise the head of Apollo's arrow that Abaris was supposed to have used for flight? Or could it represent a flying man? Or/and can we use this in place of the Celestial Gateway?

I'll try it tonight and let you know.

I tried it. Nothing happened except for some deep, pleasant but highly unlikely dreams. On that basis alone it might be jolly useful and far better than medications.

A bit poorly again so stayed at home while M went into deepest Somerset (*not* Glastonbury!) to work with Dee Banton. While I was feeling wan and weary and waiting for the match between Newcastle United and Crystal Palace on Radio 5 Live to start, I got an email from another lady feeling that she was Dion Fortune reborn. When I say I've had a lot of these recently I am not in any way sneering at any of them or dismissing the possibility, because they are all extraordinary individuals. Clearly something else is going on here so I've sent her a copy of an essay I did called 'Who or What is Dion Fortune'. Now, with only minutes left to kick-off, my legendary occult powers and highly developed clairvoyance predict 3-1 to Newcastle.

I'll let you know about that too – honestly.

It was 0-1 to Crystal Palace. Clearly I got slapped into another Parallel Life (or is it a Realm of Inane Optimism as far Newcastle United are concerned, when I made my prediction?)

Chapter 10

In the center of each whirlpool is a vortex of beauty.
Anthony T. Hincks

Of course, when we give the inner beings shape and form and even personalities like ourselves, it's only because this enables our psyches to grasp their multi-dimensional nature. There's a long and posh word to describe that but at the age of 67½ it has briefly slipped my mind. I think it might have been W. E. Butler, the magicians' magician, who once asked an elf-like being to show him what it *really* looked like, and it immediately transformed into flashes of crystalline light.

I love the image of Bel, but what would Sulis *really* look like? There are all sorts of depictions of Her on-line and most of them are very beautiful, but that's because we want to see Her like that, as expressions of our best wishes and desires.

The famous head of Minerva doesn't do it for me and I was bothered by that. As a result I found myself awake in the wee small hours on my laptop, trying to create something arty that summed her up but wasn't too human. And then it came. For me, there she is... the Eye, the Whirlpool, the powers of Water and Light. I wouldn't want Sulis to appear like that in our house though; I'd much prefer to visualise the human form of H. Mind you, I haven't had a glimpse of that form since, so maybe it *was* just our friend coming to us in spirit when she was troubled. On the other hand, the 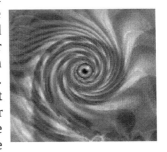 more I think of it, the full-sized full-colour original of Sulis' Eye is rather pretty - blue and silver and sparkly and twisty. Since the start of this book I've been yearning to 'see' Sulis in the psychic sense, so maybe this is how She has arranged it?

Unfortunately this greyscale version for the book reminds me a bit of the joyless, loveless entities that Kenneth Grant summoned from the Qlipothic Realms. Maybe it's the dark-light thing again but there's a difference between the purity of the Dark and the purity of the Light and the shitty, polluted, sheer uselessness of Grant's things from the Mauve Zone – whatever that is. These creatures - I can hardly call them Beings – will simply make you dirty. They exist in the U-bend of an overflowing cosmic toilet that hasn't been flushed in a million aeons.

I wrote earlier that I regretted not having met him, despite our correspondence. But looking back (*Sùil Air Ais* indeed!) I'm glad I didn't. I was too young, too impressionable, too eager to please everyone and I think the contact might have damaged me. Like many people in this odd business of magick I used to be in awe of Grant and his erudition until I felt compelled to buy his *Hecate's Fountain* quite recently. I realised then that he was making large parts of it up. There's nothing wrong in that, necessarily, as Carlos Castaneda did the same, and also my old childhood hero Lobsang Rampa – both of whom taught me hugely in differing ways. But Grant's prose is always tortuous, as if he was deliberately playing the role of the Great Adept, making sure that mere mortals could not possibly understand: esoteric obscurity masking as magickal profundity; insane cleverness that says nothing very much; numerous contradictions that he cannot be aware of. If any readers struggled with his concepts the implication was that they weren't at a high enough Grade. So I was relieved and pleased to find G.M. Kelly's essay's about Grant's books on the website 'Sword of Horus' in which he deconstructs the nonsense, shows that the gematria is often wrong, his disciples mentally unbalanced and generally rips off Aossic's mask to show someone who is more poseur than potentate.[xvi] A bit like the Fisher King, in fact.

After that rant I really need to go to some Source that is pure and healthy – and you can't get better than Ela's Well.

We had a strange morning on Winsley Hill before that though, scattering the ashes of someone who used to live in Roses Wood in the centre of the plateau. We had never met the woman, Geraldine, but her sister Jane had found a letter I had written many years ago asking about that particular area, as it formed the locale for my novella *On Winsley Hill*. After Geraldine's cremation up in Yorkshire, where she died, Jane hoped we'd scatter her ashes in the place where she had been best happy.

It was bitterly cold but sunny, and the woods were filled with bluebells. If it's possible to reincarnate as plant I want to come back as a bluebell: 11 months under the dark ground, safe and warm, then emerging with ten thousand others for a month in the Spring. And because it's illegal to pick wild flowers in this country I could feel totally protected during my brief weeks in the sun.

After that, we headed straight to Ela's Well and planned to use the little bottle that had contained the ashes to get some waters from this source. I'm sure there's symbolism in that act but I can't quite figure it out yet.

Ela's Well is lost within the Friary Woods which are perched on one side of the valley of the River Frome, which eventually merges with the Limpley Stoke valley.

When I first wrote about Ela, 3rd Countess of Salisbury and her well in 1999, I described her in *Spirits of the Stones* as 'pious and tediously devout', but I was being a bit shitty and she didn't deserve that. In the image on her personal sigillum she is tall, slim and rather lovely and looks a bit like Margaret, whom I've often thought had echoes of Ela within her. Born in Amesbury in 1187, she was in fact one of the towering female figures in the mid 13th century. Her devotion to her adored husband William Longespeé is one of the great love stories of any age and is worth researching if ever you feel jaded. Among William's countless other achievements and titles, he was given by King John the manor of Eye, in Suffolk, whose name is described in their local history books as coming from the Old English for 'island, land by water'. Apparently there was a large barrow mound surrounded by water at this spot.

Alongside William she laid the foundation stones of the new Salisbury Cathedral. After his death she held the title of High Sheriff of Wiltshire for two years then became a nun, founding Lacock Abbey in which she became Abbess in 1229, and also Hinton Priory some 16 miles away.

The well itself had a reputation for healing eye problems up to and including blindness but I feel certain it was a 'holy' well long before Ela appeared and attached her name to it. When she made a visit to bless it the Carthusian monks from the priory at the top of the hill would have been all over her on every level but the physical – and trying not to think about the hair shirts they wore beneath their habits. (They wore these as a constant reminder that physical health

and sensual pleasure are not as important as the Love of God. Even so her visit would have been as exciting to them as Tina Turner's visit was to the locals around Moyra Caldecott's place in Bath.) Ela FitzPatrick, to give her her maiden name, must have made an enormous impact on the psychic atmosphere around the well because there have been several reports of phantom monks lurking there, perhaps reliving the moment when they walked down from the priory they called *Locus Dei*, to honour her.

Call me a bit weird if you like, but I find few things more appealing than phantom monks. Of all the characters in Dion

Fortune's novels it is Hugh Paston and his alter-ego of the monk Ambrosius in *The Goat-foot God* with whom I most identify. Apart from those hair shirts I think I might have been happy as a Carthusian, but you'd have to know me today, and read about their daily routines, to see why.

Mind you, like Ambrosius' monks in the novel, they might well have been an unusual bunch on the hilltop. When the Northern Irish magician Lorraine Henry got permission to visit the (now privately owned) remains of the priory she caught a psychic whiff of alchemy in the old parts.

The first time I visited Ela's Well itself was with my fey friend of many lifetimes Annie Tod in 1999, when my life was being sucked into a terrifying maelstrom. The second time was in 2016, with Margaret, when life had become a calm and deep lake with many leafy trees peering at their own reflections on its banks. I headed off in completely the wrong direction both times and, as ever, it was the women who found the well without much trouble.

The water comes out of a narrow cleft and it's not hard to think of the Waters of the Gap here. The old stones, presumably laid and arranged by the monks, were mossed over so that the well, if you didn't know it was there, looked like a natural vulva in the hillside. I 'saw' nothing this second time but felt an enormous sense of rightness which lingered quietly over the next few days. I also apologized to Ela for being so snotty and realised that the 'white-clad women' I had glimpsed out the corner of my eye were probably shades of those white-robed Carthusian monks from the nearby priory. I had been too keen to tell a pagan yarn.

Margaret felt then, in 2016, that the whole area was alive, filled with Beings of all kinds, and that the late sun coming down through the trees was a song. I was keen to see what she might think this time, now that we were both after Sulis and any of Her tributaries on inner levels.

I know it gets tedious with the retelling and I'm conscious that old men tend to repeat the same jokes again and again, but as I stood by the car I felt exasperated that Margaret was battling through the trees in completely the wrong direction. And of course it was completely the right direction.

To tell the truth it was difficult to get to the well this time. A lot of small trees had blown down and had created a cat's cradle of branches and trunks. It almost needed a machete to get there.

The first time I visited in 1999 water had poured out with some vigour and the stones around it glistened. The second time in 2016 there was a strong outpouring from amid the slightly mossed surrounding stones and I had had vivid dreams of reaching into the pool at the bottom to find treasure. This time, 2019, there was only the merest trickle of water and the stones were so covered in thick moss that, unless you knew, no-one would ever recognise this as a well at all. I took several photos but they weren't very good and not worth reproducing here. Perhaps Ela wants her well to remain hidden forever. I used that silly little water-testing device and found that the trickle registered a purity of 00.0.

Even so... There was still a marked atmosphere in this spot, helped by what Margaret told me were masses of wild garlic, primroses and wood anemones – not to mention an ocean of bluebells. It felt unvisited, elemental and enveloping.

The sun came through the tall trees again from the white sky above and the wind suddenly picked up – not in a rage, but as means of speaking to us, I think, shushing and shushing, and telling stories that better seers than us would have been able to understand in ages past.

We both said our private things to Sulis and I apologised to Ela once again for the undeserved crass comments of earlier years, added nice things about her husband William, and had the sense in return that I had finally put something right.

Then I filled the little bottle which had contained Geraldine's ashes and found a small shell at the bottom in the rivulet, and would add both to our pond at home with appropriate words.

If we had come later in the year the undergrowth would have become impenetrable. I felt that no-one else would ever come here again in my lifetime, and Ela's waters would be happy with that...

Chapter 11

Anger is like flowing water; there's nothing wrong with it as long as you let it flow. Hate is like stagnant water; anger that you denied yourself the freedom to feel, the freedom to flow; water that you gathered in one place and left to forget. Stagnant water becomes dirty, stinky, disease-ridden, poisonous, deadly; that is your hate. On flowing water travels little paper boats; paper boats of forgiveness. Allow yourself to feel anger, allow your waters to flow, along with all the paper boats of forgiveness. Be human.

C. JoyBell C

I realised that there are countless people today who night be regarded as active, practising priests and priestesses of Sulis. They don't wear robes, don't use incantations or invocations, rarely work in any kind of organised groups and are best recognised by nothing more dramatic than their use of a forked hazel twig. They are of course the dowsers.

I've never been able to get any kind of dowsing device to work, though Margaret can. I only really became aware of dowsing when (goodness knows how) I stumbled upon Guy Underwood's groundbreaking book *The Pattern of the Past* when it first came out, in 1974 I think. I was in Kentucky at the time and was vaguely excited by his notions though I didn't understand much of his terminology. He argued that our ancestors patterned Stonehenge and other sites as they did because they could detect a beneficial Earth Force of underground water lines that dictated the layout of these monuments as markers for subterranean streams. He also asserted that medieval cathedrals were similarly aligned, and thus felt he had deduced some of the secrets of the Freemasons.

Reading it again last night, I still don't understand much of his terminology and I think that modern dowsers have modified these. But the ideas that flow behind the awkward concepts are thrilling. He quoted the work of two French archaeologists Louis Merle and

Charles Diot who had published papers in 1933 and 1935 arguing that all prehistoric burial places and similar stone structures in France were **surrounded** [his italics] by underground streams and that the famous stone avenue at Carnac – which consists of great stones set in a number of parallel lines several miles long – is aligned upon underground streams running parallel with each other. He then enthused about Captain Robert Boothby RN who published an article *The Religion of the Stone Age* in which he claimed that all barrows and other prehistoric sites were **crossed** [ditto] by underground streams and that every long barrow had an underground stream running its full length.

He felt that as water was the most sacred substance of the old religions, it followed that certain 'blind springs' and waterlines determined the exact position of the altar in the oldest churches. But dowsing beyond the Christian newcomers to this world, back to the most ancient of days he noted: 'I became absorbed by the extreme importance of the serpent symbol in prehistoric religions, and the subsequent emergence of the serpent as a god believed to control fertility.' Well, Bel's beard is writhing with two serpents, and Minerva was also linked with them.

In writing his book about the universal and all-important influence of Water, Underwood is clearly on fire, although he knew that it might take a long while before his ideas would gain acceptance. As he became accomplished at dowsing himself, after long practice, he stated:

> Diviners agree that they are not affected by surface water...
> and that the only water which affects them and causes their
> rods to move is an underground stream, that is to say
> underground water in motion, under pressure, subject to
> friction and connected ultimately with the sea.

I think in writing that he anticipated Alick Bartholomew's ideas about *yin* and *yang* by a few decades.

In one of the strange swirlings of happenstance that have marked my life, I was startled to find 20 years later when I re-read the book, that many of his early dowsing experiments were done in the Bath/Winsley/Bradford-on-Avon area (in one case at the very bottom of my street) and that he lived in the Belcombe area of BoA, though not in the nearby Court itself. In my list of people that I regret not having met, I'll remove Aossic and put Guy Underwood in his place.

In dowsing for Sulis' watery energies he also found, in the years 1942-47, a stone circle with a central stone seat in No Man's Land, Conkwell. Although people since have questioned its existence because there is almost no trace of this now, I remember it being largely intact in 1986, exactly as he described it in the *Wiltshire Archaeological Magazine*. Local lore has it that Arthur Guirdham had his first visions here, which led him to write *The Cathars and Reincarnation*. And I think it was somewhere around here that I was once bound to a standing stone as a Willing Sacrifice and had a flint knife stabbed into my heart.

And Underwood also found an extraordinary complex at the adjoining Inwoods that seems, from the size of it, to have been a pre-eminent centre in Neolithic times, with eight miles of linear mounds, all aligned on aquastats and appearing to be processional ways. He also found several barrows, one of which contained two crouched burials and a gold sun disk.

We'll come back to that 'sun disk' and the local veneration for the historically dubious but magickally potent figure of Katharine later...

It's another glorious day. I'm sitting in the garden watching the disk of the actual sun curving over it. Is that Bel? Or is that Horus? Or Ra-Horakhty? - as Crowley and Laura Jennings-Yorke (as she became) would have termed it. Prince, our enormously fat pigeon bounces across the patio in search of more seed. Margaret reckons it's actually a dove, but I don't think so and I love her too much to google her wrong. She is wrestling at the moment with very large sheet of ultra thin weed-suppressant fabric. The light breezes catches in the folds and wraps it around her like a witch's cloak. She wants to put this down in narrow strips and create something wondrous along our borders. She is now completely en-wrapped and looking less like a witch in her cloak and more like something from *The Mummy*. Despite Beltaine coming up fast I really must put Bel and Sulis aside for a moment and attend to the truly important things of life here on earth...

*Let **me** do that, my little chickadee...*

I was quite thrilled to find (via Google of course) that the Bible states in Revelations 19:9 that the Whore of Babylon dwells on seven hills. Well, the Bible can't be wrong can it? And Bath lies within seven hills! Because Margaret is off to Brussels tomorrow I plan to drive among some of these hills in search of St Catherine's Well, but I'll certainly keep an eye out for the Whore. And give her total respect, as any human with a heart must do.

St Catherine's Valley is a large and lush area of Special Scientific Interest which stretches south-west of the village of Marshfield, and down into the eastern fringe of Bath. It was designated SSI because in 1927 someone found a large naturalised population of Dragon's Teeth (*Tetragonolobus maritimus*), a species not native to Britain. I've no idea what Dragon's Teeth is or are, and you can tell I've plundered *Wikipedia* to which I donate the occasional fiver.

I do know Marshfield though and it is a strange town where I once had very clear memories of a (very ordinary, hard and very dreary) past life as a farm hand. It also has its Mummers.

The Marshfield Paper Boys, as they call themselves, perform a traditional mummers play every Boxing Day in the village. It's a typical hero/combat play involving a sword-fight and the revival of the defeated protagonist by the Doctor; other characters include Saucy Jack and Father Beelzebub. I'd enjoy playing that last one, I think.

The players wear costumes covered in strips of paper (hence their name) and perform in a serious manner handed down over the generations. There is evidence of mummers' plays since circa 1141, and though this one is a revival of a lapsed custom, one of the revivalists had been in the original group as a child before its demise, so there is a direct connection with the old ways and this makes the event unique.

To me, the little town has a deliciously odd, almost witchy atmosphere. They could have filmed *The Wicker Man* here with none of the problems they had up in Galloway. I also learned that Dylan Thomas and Caitlin once lived in Marshfield, though I've been unable to find out exactly where. They would certainly have hit the three pubs and though a teetotaller I've been in all of them just to get a glimpse. When William Gray wrote about cycling to the Rollright Stones to work magic ('*Without* the 'k' please Alan', as he was wont to insist), he felt that the circle almost sent out a homing beacon as he approached. I sometimes feel that with Marshfield. And although I aim to get to the Well, I might also find myself being magnetised toward that odd little town.

I had dropped off Margaret at the train station in Chippenham (a busy town known to the locals as 'Nam) and decided that instead of coming home to do Timeless Prose I would go to St Catherine's Valley by myself.

The fact is, the balmy and unnatural weather of the last few weeks seemed to have ended this morning. Rain fell heavily and it was a miserable day. I thought I would 'do' Catherine myself, and also keep an eye out for the first female or male I saw on entering the complex of Bath's seven hills. This would surely be the Whore of Babalon according to my researches.

It had been some 15 years since I had last driven along this valley, a perfect example of Deepest England that is every bit as compelling as La France Profonde across the Channel. It warns as you enter that there is only a Single Track Road, with Passing Places, although I knew that the latter were few and far between. Not Suitable For Large Vehicles another sign adds. And a little further along, if this still hasn't put you off, a final sign saying; Pedestrians Have Priority. Large Vehicles Get Stuck After This Point.

If you're a passenger and trust your driver along the narrowest of roads, steepest of hills and endless blind bends, the scenery of the valley is sublime. If you're the actual driver it can bring moments when you wish you hadn't bothered. Fortunately, I didn't meet another car coming from the opposite direction. To create a crass metaphor, I can see why the valley was named after a determined virgin: it is not easy to penetrate once you have found it, and the lush folds don't offer welcome.

St Catherine's Court is a Grade 1 listed monument, a fine example of a late Tudor and early Jacobean Court in Renaissance style, with Benedictine origins dating back to 950 CE. It is built of the local and lovely Cotswold stone under a stone-tiled roof, with stone mullion and leaded light windows and retains original fires and features that date back to the reign of Henry VIII and beyond. There are large and numerous signs saying that this is Private Property and no-one can come in. However, the grounds also contain the Church of St Catherine and anyone can come in there.

The church is a 'chapel-of-ease'. I didn't know it, but a chapel-of-ease is a church building built for the attendance of those who cannot easily reach their parish church. In this case, their parish church is in Bath, which is only a couple of miles away if that, but it must have been the devil's own job to get out of that valley. It is a tiny church, seating 50 at the very most, and was also used as a retreat for the monks of Bath though there didn't seem to be any phantom examples floating around. The windows in the chancel contain medieval glass.

The nave and tower date from the thirteenth century, and it was embellished by several generations of the families who have lived at the Court, including the seventeenth-century Blanchard family tomb.

For me, the rain was coming down in sheets and I was cold and a bit lost on other levels than the physical. I just wanted to find St Catherine's Well, which I did, tucked away between house and church.

Sulis might have been soaking me from the heavens above, but the well of the virgin was dry. Apparently the true Source was on the hill above; the waters had once poured down through conduits to splash out here, with steps for the pilgrims to kneel before it and be lubricated. But having been diagnosed with angina a little while before and worried about having a dicky ticker I wasn't gonna go hill-walking just yet. Margaret would have killed me if I'd tried it by myself and had a heart attack.

The valley did grace me with an adequate lay-by opposite the Court which enabled me to get my breath back, study the road map (I'd left the OS at home) and see if I could glimpse the Whore of Babalon anywhere. I'm not sneering. If I can be prodded on my shoulder by an Alien in Trowbridge then this was a very modest ask. St. Catherine's Court used to be the home of the actress Jane Seymour who had a certain slight fame in *Live and Let Die* as the tarot-reading virgin priestess of Obeah, called Solitaire, who can see both the future and remote events. Once she had sex with James Bond, though, she lost all her powers.

I think she's long gone from the place but a glimpse of her might have ticked all the boxes. As it turned out I didn't see a single soul, so if the Whore of Babylon *did* live among the hills of Bath it was in my head only. I can think of worse places.

Mind you, just as Sulis has different names and different forms through the ages, Jane Seymour's real name is Joyce Penelope Wilhelmina Frankenberg. Because she was born in the same year as me, I suspect she probably doesn't look like that now.

There was a strong pull to go on from that little lay-by, up and over the hills to Marshfield, but the even smaller side road plunged down like a ski-slope first and seemed to be flooded at the bottom. If Margaret had been there I'd have risked it, but as it was, I just wanted to get home and have a quick nap, then put Katharine to bed, so to speak.

I wrote earlier about Guy Underwood, who found various ancient sites by means of dowsing. In one of them, on the plateau of Winsley Hill, amid the old forest surrounding a property now known as Inwoods, he helped excavate a burial mound in which an extraordinary 'sun disk' was found.

It was made in about 2,400 BCE, soon after the sarsen stones were put up at Stonehenge and is one of only six sun-disks ever discovered, plus one of the earliest metal objects found in Britain. They found it along with a pottery beaker, flint arrowheads and fragments of the skeleton of an adult male.

A couple of years ago I wrote to owner of Inwoods and he invited us around to wander in the woods, soaking up whatever atmospheres we might find. There wasn't much to see, very little left of Jug's Grave, as the mound is called, but I'm glad we made the effort. Although he kept the sun-disk upstairs in a safe he didn't offer to show it to us, and seemed more excited about the bomb crater left in the woods from the Second World War. After his death, he donated the disk to Devizes Museum which contains some of the finest Bronze Age artefacts in the country. I could spend hours sitting in front of the case, wishing that disk was mine. The curators keep a close eye on me.

The Museum describes it thus:

> The sun-disk is a thin embossed sheet of gold with a cross at the centre, surrounded by a circle. Between the lines of both the cross and the circle are fine dots which glint in sunlight. The disc is pierced by two holes that may have been used to sew the disc to a piece of clothing or a head-dress, and may have been used in pairs. Until recently it has been thought that early Bronze Age gold may have come from Ireland, but a new scientific technique developed at Southampton University is hinting that the gold may have come from Cornwall.

To me, this is an extraordinary item of High Magick. I think it must have been regarded as such when it first made - perhaps even more so. In the inner stories and yarns that I'm always creating within my mind, this disk has somehow burned itself into the collective souls of that area, down through the millennia, influencing how they came to accept the later images of Saint Katharine of Alexandria – Catherine of the Wheel - as their own.

Listen, they must have thought, when they heard her story from the priests, *She is of the Wheel!* They would never have seen the actual sun disk, which had been buried thousands of years before, but somehow it was burned into the psychic equivalents of DNA and place-memory. Which is why Katharine is omnipresent throughout that small area and why Cattern's Day was once more important to them than Christmas.

And also, I see now as I write, there is the equi-armed Cross of Bride within the Wheel, giving me a clear connection between Bridget/Bride/Bridey and Katharine that I couldn't get before. And before and beyond *them*, the link across the valley and through the hill to Sulis, from whom all flows.

Oh I know, I know... There probably isn't such a thing as 'psychic equivalents of DNA and place-memory'. This is all a bit far-fetched if you don't live in this area and don't have my life, but it works for me. It hydrates me, spiritually. If I hadn't been drawn to the Waters of the Gap in the first place and found myself calling on Sulis then I would never have been able to see any of this. She must have had her Eye on me all the time, without me knowing.

Thank you for that Sulis!

Chapter 12

Came in close, I heard a voice/ Standing, stretching every
nerve/I had to listen, had no choice/I did not believe the
information/Just had to trust imagination

Peter Gabriel

The weather front today, 27th April, has been named as Storm
Hannah. 85 mph gales in some parts of the country, but not too
extreme here. I guess that the accompanying heavy rain is also part
of Sulis's Mysteries of Baptism. Margaret was once told by the soul-
reader Julie Wise that in a previous life I'd been a Chinese Weather
Magician. I have no notions about that but I like the myth of it;
we've a few yarns to tell in that direction too, but they'll wait for
another project. I won't go weird and try to stop this weather but I do
hope it clears up for our trip up Solsbury Hill.

She's in bed at the moment as she didn't get back from Brussels
until late last night and is knackered. I take her de-caff coffee in a big
mug. The wind shakes the windows.

'The garden will love this,' she says.

'But listen, you've just *got* to hear this...' I insist. I have to read
her two wee snippets from a book that I stumbled on yesterday.

The book is simply called *Penetration* by Ingo Swann. Swann,
who died in 2013, has been described by many others as a 'top psi-
spy' because of his work on behalf of various intelligence agencies,
including the CIA, in 'black projects' that have only recently been
revealed. Quite apart from his unwitting physical contacts with extra-
terrestrials that were living among us in the 1970s, he provided two
brief paragraphs that helped clarify my modest attempts to find Sulis.
When asked by the mysterious Mr. Axelrod if he was reading the
Akashic record 'or something like that', Swann answered:

> No, not exactly. Some kind of species memory storage –
> maybe at the DNA molecular level. I know this idea makes
> scientists throw up, but so does any aspect of Psi.

So perhaps my own clumsy notion regarding the survival of the gold sun-disk in the *tribal* DNA memory storage in that area, is perhaps not so far fetched.

But there was also another couple of brief paragraphs that I found quite charming and also helped illuminate many of the areas discussed in this book:

> In our research of remote-viewing capacities, we have learned that when viewers 'see' something they don't understand, they explain it in ways that make sense to them. For example, to a viewer who has never seen an actual atomic reactor, what they are sensing can be described as a teapot, both of which are hot and 'cook'... The psychic subject in remote-viewing a site with an atomic reactor may well overlay the impressions with a 'teapot' or a 'furnace' because these are the memory images which come closest to what is being psychically sensed....People fill in the unknown with what fits with THEIR known.[xvii]

I suppose that is why I had the fevered images of H when I first tried to 'see' Sulis, and also might explain the bizarre appearance underground of Robin Hood, in the style of Kevin Costner. Robin Hood is my 'teapot'. Gawd knows what, if anything, my mind was really touching upon then.

Incidentally, now that the wind is beginning to drop and the sun is coming out, here is another large hint...

Although the American and Russian programmes involving 'psychic spying' have been fairly well-documented, few people know that the United Kingdom also had their own covert organisation. In the 1960s the Ministry of Defence invested £18,000 in a highly secret programme to test the efficacy of Remote Viewing. This department, working under the aegis of MI5, was known as Defence Intelligence 15. I used this as the basis of my novel *Twisted Light*, featuring Kaspar O'Malley, and had him living in Bratton near Cat's Well. Kaspar's persona is largely my own, though only

Margaret sees this. Which is why the doppelgänger's appearance that day when we went to Cat's Well startled me so much.

Don't breathe a word of this. And if you buy a copy, I'll meet you in Amenti and give you the grand tour.

Beltaine is rapidly approaching and I rather hope to get this published on that date, for obvious reasons. I feel that because we start searching in a deep, wet cavern, we must finish it on a high and hard hill, thus bringing primal Female and Male events into some sort of climax.

Plus there's a cafe in Batheaston, at the foot of Solsbury Hill, that we still haven't visited that looks wonderful and doesn't even advertise on-line.

I've done all the preparation, have long since had the Ordinance Survey map, and have identified the two springs marked as being near the summit of the hill. I want water from one of them. Plus I've also made a small talisman using Bel's image that I plan to push into the ground, if it feels right to do so, as a payment.

Also, I haven't given up hope of glimpsing the Whore of Babylon, with Margaret's help this time. We've decided that from the moment we park the car in Batheaston, until we get to the summit of the hill, the first person to make eye-contact with either of us, or even nod or say hello, is the Whore in question. Particularly, I wanted to get some sense of Bladud up there and perhaps the teensiest hint of Abaris, if indeed the two were connected.

If Bladud had historical existence (and I believe he did) he would certainly have spent time in what must have been the pre-eminent hill-fort in this area. And if he wanted to actually fly from anywhere, then surely the angled slopes of Solsbury Hill would have been a more likely starting place than off the castle walls of Trinovantum. Less chance of a disastrous crash; less chance of egg on his face if he failed. One of the things I've noticed in my long life is that high-flying Adepts (and I've met more than a few of them) are just as likely to make absolute tits of themselves and crash to earth as heavily as the rest of us, no matter how high-flown their inner contacts might be.

I think it symbolic that a man named after an angel (Peter Gabriel) felt himself spoken to by an unknown Being after he left the band Genesis and so created his hit single, named after the hill itself. Was it Bladud who spoke? Record companies can get pretty fierce about quoting lyrics for nowt, so if you're interested in the whole thing you might like to google them yourself. Why can't Peter Gabriel be one of the 'celebrities' that come to me in dreams? He'd be a whole lot more appropriate than Kevin Costner in his Robin Hood outfit, who for some shallow reason Margaret fancies rotten. (I've explained that actually he's just a teapot, but it doesn't put her off.) In his song, Gabriel he mentions an eagle that flew out of the night. For this last trip of ours, I'd settle for the hawk of Horus.

Solsbury Hill is a small flat-topped hill and the site of an Iron Age hill fort that was once occupied between 300 BCE and 100 BCE, but you'd have to have a keen eye to notice any traces of that today. Although visible from quite some distance around it is not a large hill and only rises to 625 feet.

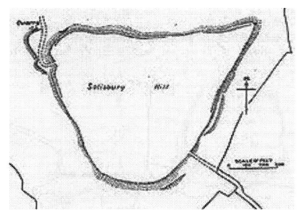

It is regarded as one of the possible sites of the legendary Battle of Badon, thought to have been fought in the late 5th or early 6th century between the Celtic Brits (whom we now think of as Welsh) and the Anglo-Saxons (whom we now call the English). It was a major victory for the Britons and stopped the encroachment of the Anglo-Saxon kingdoms for a period. However a dozen other places around the country have claimed the site of Badon as theirs, mainly because the Britons were supposedly led by King Arthur. The Welsh, Scots, English and Bretons all claim him for their own.

The name 'Solsbury' has no connection with the town of Salisbury and you'd need to have an acute ear to notice the difference in pronunciations. The name may be derived from Sulis, although Moyra Caldecott disputes this and I'm inclined to agree with her. I'm not sure if anyone has ever argued simply for it being named by the Romans as the hill of Sol, the sun god. The eponymous hero of my novel *du Lac* insisted that the buns famous in Bath today, in the grossly over-priced tea-shop and tourist trap known as Sally Lunn's, were derived from the days of the Legions: a whole round bun was a Sol and a half bun was a Lune; hence the name *sol-et-lune*. (Du Lac, incidentally, was a very powerful, very real inner contact who hated the name Lancelot as he felt it was akin to a 'slave name'. I liked him a lot, and given the Watery nature of the present book I'd rather hoped he might appear again; so far, not even the smallest droplet of du Lac's energy has landed on my brow.)

After all, the Legions were drawn to Bath because, like Rome, it was surrounded by seven hills, and they would certainly have named them accordingly and linked them to the heavens. For those who might want to create an earth/sky/planetary thing like Mary Caine and Katharine Maltwood did with their Glastonbury zodiacs, then these seven hills are: Combe Down, Odd Down, Lansdowne, Claverton Down, Bathampton Down, Bathwick Hill and Solsbury Hill itself.

Caine and Maltwood's books are fascinating and groundbreaking but personally I feel that everyone can find their own 'Temple of the Stars' in the land around them, in whatever country they live. The effort alone can be transformative. In a bizarre and compelling personal quest Graham K. Griffiths, in his limited-edition book *Behold Jerusalem*, argues that the entire landmass of Britain and

Ireland comprises ALL the constellations and is trying '... via the universal language of mythology, to warn us that all creation stands at this moment upon a monumental brink. One of either pending catastrophe or, if we have the perception, one over which we can make an evolutionary leap.' Honestly, it's as outlandish as Rendel Harris' book about Nephthys and Isis in Wiltshire, but of the two I much prefer the latter because Griffiths has clearly never even heard of the recently anointed Holy City of Holt.

I must confess that I was a bit worried my supposedly dicky heart might cause me problems climbing the hill. Then again I was inspired by Moyra Caldecott who, writing in her 80s, described how she had climbed GlasVegasbury Tor while having an angina attack 20 years before. I was damned certain that we would take 'our' sacred hill. In the event I shot up the long, long approach slope like a greyhound. Margaret, who goes to the gym and works out every day, followed on behind panting. 'You're a freak' she said, not for the first time.

Mind you, we both agreed that the first person we saw on the way really was the Whore of Babylon, who smiled at us hugely as if she was privy to our little joke. In person she was fair-haired, middle aged and looked a lot like H. She also had a muzzled whippet on a lead. The name 'whippet', it has been argued, is derived from 'Wepawet', or Anubis, the Opener of the Way.

Hmmmm I thought.

At the gate to the actual summit was a sign advising that between 1st March and 31st July all walkers should keep to the perimeter to avoid disturbing or damaging the ground-nesting Skylarks, which had become an endangered species.

We held the talisman I had made, imbued it with whatever *mana* we might be able to conjure, and pushed it deep into the earth as payment. Then we got up to explore.

Needless to say it was Margaret who immediately found the springs as if drawn to them by their own homing beacons. They were – what's the term - 'capped', where they emerged from the solid white rock, and cattle troughs placed to receive the flow. At the centre of the hill, near the trig point, I used Bill Gray's simple Elemental invocation:

Thou Sun, thou Sky
Thou Earth, thou Sea
I am the living centre of thy circled Cross
Live equally in me...

Then as we encircled the hilltop, widdershins, I verbally thanked all those people who had once lived and loved and fought here, and all the energies/entities that may have brought us – *summoned* us more likely – into this area to meet and work magick.

Margaret followed behind me physically but was far ahead of me on all inner levels, working with her own contacts. One day she might talk about that herself.

On the north side, on a slightly lower terrace, we were both struck by a lovely little maze. Well, not so much a maze as a labyrinth, an ancient design that you can trace inward and outward, which we did.

In an odd way it expressed all the inner work we had been doing for the past few months – possibly for the past myriad lifetimes.

When we stood together at the centre we toasted Sulis and Bladud and offered our own libation, thinking that in 10,000 years it will find its way down through the strata toward the centre of Bath and re-emerge, hot and steaming and full of stories for the likes of us.

Once we had finished we completed the circuit and strolled back down feeling rather pleased with ourselves. I didn't see any Hawks. Then again, if Horus was behind me as the witch woman said, then I wasn't likely to. The only down-side was that the amazing looking cafe on Batheaston high street was only open Tuesday to Friday, so we had to go to Morrisons instead.

Which rather brings us to the end of what we want to do. If we tried to include all the wells, streams, ponds, rivers and their associated myths (if any) modern and ancient, in this area, then we'd end up with a never-ending story. You'd all go glassy-eyed by the time you got to Chapter 418.

Chapter 13

I am part of the sun as my eye is part of me. That I am part of the earth my feet know perfectly, and my blood is part of the sea. There is not any part of me that is alone and absolute except my mind, and we shall find that the mind has no existence by itself, it is only the glitter of the sun on the surfaces of the water.

D.H. Lawrence

We began this book hoping to find Sulis. For myself, I was rather hoping that She would manifest visibly: a shining presence at the end of our bed, bestowing blessings and adding a few apports falling down from the ceiling and making us gasp. Alas, nothing of that sort happened. It's possible that Sulis may have used the image of H during that fevered night but I'm not totally convinced. However, I've become quite certain that when I felt an inner pressure to get up in the wee small hours to fiddle and faff about with the image and photo editing software on my pc, that something akin to Sulis's 'true' form was given to me. This powerful Eye within the Whirlpool may be a bit uncomfortable for others, but they must find their own image. As I said earlier, the only sad thing is that the greyscale version used within this text looks a bit forbidding. The sparkly original - all azure and turquoise and deep blues and silver curls – invokes Her for me. If any reader wants me to email that as an attachment I'll be more than happy to do so and I don't need to know whether they use PayPal before I send it.

Quite apart from those visual manifestations, if that's what they were, I still do have a fairly continuous sense of connection with *Something*. It is benign and omnipresent and doesn't seem to demand anything from me, unlike those bloody Templars I worked with and for last year. But perhaps this is likely to do with my awareness of the extent to which Water is pre-eminent within this world. If All is One, as I keep saying, then perhaps I might adapt that lovely quote from Dion Fortune's *The Sea Priestess* to read: 'All the Rivers are one River, all the Lakes are one Lake, and there is but one Ocean.'

And of course we are part of this. The average adult human body is 50-65% water, and the percentage in infants is much higher, typically around 75-78% water. The percentage of water on the Earth's surface is about 71%, and you can see the parallel.

Although this book is just about finished, I don't think Sulis is about to go away yet and for that I'm right glad. She doesn't make me powerful, or particularly wise, but I do feel a bit more connected with that indefinable *Something,* even if it is only akin to the glittering of sun on the surfaces of the water.

As for...

Bel...

I do love his face. I'm glad I gave him eyes. Maybe he thinks *I'm* Sulis!

I really don't know Who or What this face represents but I'm not sure it is Pontus, as Paul Dunne argues. Bladud? Abaris the Hyperborean? Horus? Bel?

There are a few still small voices out there that argue that *this* is Sulis. In this strange Age that is unfolding now when people are identifying as non-binary, transitioning, gender queer, bi-sexual, tri-sexual, androgymous, pan-gender and many more that I don't really understand, we might not want to view dear Bel as singularly male. I think everyone has to get right into that amazing face, look into Bel's eyes and decide for themselves.

Bladud...

Was that really an appearance by him as I was lambasting the Fisher King? I think it was. I wish I could be more exciting and say that he now bursts into my mind and brings me messages from beyond the stars, or even from beyond the naff 'celebrities' that have plagued my dream states, but he doesn't. Not does the hugely intriguing figure of Abaris, his alter ego or historical self, even wink at me. But it's still early days.

I would add, though, that this doesn't mean I've failed or that such energies/entities (I still don't know what they are) don't exist. All sorts of other things have gone on in both of our lives during this period; events too cumbersome and complicated to describe here. Although they haven't seemed to be obviously related to Sulis and Bel and the priest Bladud, perhaps these energies and events flowed through channels that were subtly and secretly cut by them.

Minerva and Katharine...

The image and myth of Minerva, still does nothing for me. That's possibly because the Mithraic tone of that 'other' life of mine doesn't gel. I use the term 'other' life deliberately because I sometimes think that there is no past/present/future and that it's all happening in the infinite Now, but I won't be dogmatic about this. As the lovely sage Judy Hall pointed out to me, sometimes the *only* explanation for the things she has experienced is reincarnation. And just for ease of discussion, it's simpler to talk about these things as historical previous lives in the reincarnational sense, than bang on about the 'other' parts of me existing Now.

Katharine on the other hand really does gel. I've no intention of creating anything Christian or devotional around the idea of **St.** Katharine of Alexandria. In fact I'll drop the 'Saint' part now because I get a certain frisson from the knowledge that the name means Pure, which takes me straight back to the clean light of Sulis in the Source. I think that Hypatia of Alexandria, who really did exist, and whose name means Highest, Supreme, is a nice match. On November 25th I will astonish Margaret by asking her to show me how to use our cooker, get her to describe where certain of the ingredients can be found in Tescos and what they actually look like, then I will make a tray full of magnificent Cattern Cakes. I might even scatter them with those hundreds-and-thousands that I can eat whole boxes of. They will be far better and far healthier than those 'Cakes of Light' that Crowley recommended, that were composed of meal, honey, oil and certain female bodily fluids.

So, to conclude, let me tell you all how to become a fully initiated priest or priestess of Sulis…

- First, you need to have the Intent.
- Second, you get a clean glass and go to the kitchen sink (sacred places, kitchens!).
- Third, you must visualise Sulis in whatever way works for you as the Ultimate Source for the water in your tap.
- Fourth, you must fill your glass, visualising the water as a stream of purest Light.
- Fifth, visualise your glass as filled with brilliant, glowing energy.
- Sixth, lift your glass and toast Sulis, then drink it, preferably in one glug.
- Seventh, visualise your whole body as being filled with Sulis's light.

Erm… that's all. You are now fully initiated and can begin.

DON'T imagine that because Sulis is universal yet so little known, that out of the Waters of the Gap you can create a Gap in the Market.

DON'T end up putting Her on mugs or t-shirts or hats with a stupid logo saying: *I ♥ Sulis* and doing blogs and vlogs and weekend retreats in which all major credit cards are accepted. The goddess Herself will be supremely indifferent to all this tosh, but dear old Uncle Alan will be hugely disappointed.

Really, you are surrounded by Sulis. She is within and without. She is everywhere. Only you can find Her. Start looking, and keep an Eye out wherever you go. She will give you all sorts of adventures, often without realising. She come to you in all sorts of guises and wearing unusual masks. You will find you own Names and Images that will make more sense than any of the ones we've suggested. And hopefully you will learn not to become pompous, as happens with so many mystics and magicians who become convinced that the Sources they tap are the only ones worth drinking from.

To which we can only, now, reveal our own *Truest* Selves on the next page and hope that you can all cope and won't tell a soul...

Walter, Prince of Softies

Beryl the Peril

ISIS AND NEPHTHYS IN WILTSHIRE AND ELSEWHERE

BY
RENDEL HARRIS

[Reproduced from the pamphlet written in 1938, with an article about St Catherine by E.F. Wills. Their images may not reproduce very well here]

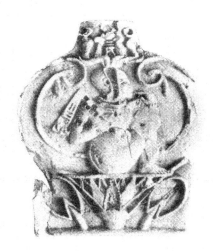

ISIS AND NEPHTHYS IN WILT SHIRE AND ELSEWHERE

We have before us a reproduction of what may be described as one of the most exciting recoveries of Palestine exploration. A stray allusion in the Old Testament informed us that one of the kings of Israel built for himself an ivory palace on the hill of Samaria. No one, I suppose, expected that fragments of this wonderful ivory palace would ever come to light.

A band of workers, indeed, both from England and America were conducting excavations at the capital city of King Ahab, with very good results for the most part, but with some sense of disappointment, for I suppose that what they were trying to find with the utmost zeal and expectation was the burial chambers of the kings of Israel. Somewhere in the vicinity of Samaria there will yet be found a magnificent array of carved sarcophagi representing the ancient dynasty of Israel from the time of Solomon onward. These have not yet been found, but what was found was the remains of the ivory palace of King Ahab to which the stray reference was made in the First Book of Kings[1]. Broken fragments of ivory came to light, and it was possible to reconstruct from these a lovely Egyptian monument representing Isis and Nephthys adoring a pillar between them which stood for the great god Osiris. To this was added an ivory figure of Horus, the child of Isis.

So here we have before us a lovely work of Egyptian art produced for King Ahab by artists who must have come from Egypt and brought their materials with them, the ivory having come from as far away as the First Cataract of the Nile. We open our eyes very wide with wonder. No scholar ever suspected anything of the kind as far as religion goes, for these carvings are profoundly religious. We only thought of Ahab as one of the bad kings of Israel with a wife who was even worse than himself. It was not the Baal of Ahab and Jezebel that came to light.

On the other hand we were undeceived also as to the value of the work of King Ahab as artist and architect. Before the Egyptian figures came to light, one school of critics spoke of Samaria as a city

---

1   1 Kings 22

of palaces under Assyrian influence. Assyria now takes second rank before Egyptian monuments and Egyptian religion and whatever is involved therein. For our purposes what has appeared is undoubtedly a wave of Egyptian religion in Samaria itself. The religion of Samaria has been overstated in terms of a distracted ditheism, the battle-ground between Jehovah and the Tyrian Baal. Ahab himself may probably be better explained from his intrigues with the Egyptian Foreign Office than by speculations as to the supremacy of Tyre at that end of the Mediterranean. Four great Egyptian deities, at least, have sprung into life in Samaria itself. This was not dead religion with figures taken out of a picture book. lsis and Nephthys, Osiris and Horus stand for religion in an aggressive form. The deities themselves have turned migrants. Our reason for putting the matter in this way is that we want to speculate on the existence of similar religious phenomena elsewhere. Can we find anything of the kind in Britain? And to put it simply, without any ivory palace to assist us, can we find lsis and Nephthys in Wiltshire, to take a single instance?

If it was difficult to believe that the appearance of the Osirian group in Ahab's palace at Samaria was devoid either of political or religious significance, may we not say something similar in cases where we recover the names of the deities even though we have not yet succeeded in excavating their sculptured forms?

In the case of lsis and Nephthys we have not only those names which are familiar to us in the classical tradition, especially the name of lsis which is of very frequent occurrence, but we have also a variety of names which conveyed the two great goddesses under a double appellation. For example, they are known as Merti the two beloved women, as Haiti, the two weeping women, and as Remuti, another title for the two weeping women which comes to us through Pharmouthi, (paremuti), the last of the Egyptian months. And then last of all there is a name which we might easily have missed, though its occurrence is very frequent, the two goddesses being represented under the sign *Tcher,* the 'Great Tcher' standing for lsis, and the 'Little Tcher' for her sister Nephthys[2].

---

2 See Budge, *Lexicon*

Let us now see how these names have impressed themselves on the geographical conscience on either side of the Atlantic. We will begin with--

$$ISIS + NEPHTHYS = HAITI \text{ (or HEYTI)}.$$

The discovery of the meaning of this West lndian name came about in the following way, as l have several times already described. We had been following Columbus in his voyages from the Canaries to the Bahamas, and then, under the guidance of friendly lndians (almost all lndians at that time were friendly) from the Bahamas to the greater islands of the Caribbean Sea and in particular to the island of Haiti. Columbus took possession of this island in the name of his great patrons Ferdinand and lsabella, and said that it should be called Hispaniola or Little Spain. The lndians, however, said its name was Haiti; and so powerfully was this name established among them that when Columbus returned on a subsequent voyage he found that the new name, Hispaniola, was oft the map, and the older name Haiti or Heyti had not been removed.

lt did not occur to me at that time to ask the meaning of the supposed lndian name. We ought, of course, to have recognised that it was a truly Egyptian word and stood for a dual feminine implying 'two weeping women' who could in Egyptian be nothing else than lsis and Nephthys. We do not blame Columbus for not knowing the meaning of the word.

We ourselves came to the interpretation thereof quite gradually by noticing that in the south-west of the county of Wilts., there was a village with the name of Heytesbury. Here was the mysterious Heyti with an Anglo-Saxon tail-piece, and we had to explain whether we were dealing with a pair of coincident names or whether it was possible that there could be an underground and undersea connection between them. As we could not imagine a philological tunnel between Wiltshire and the West Indies, we waited for the light to dawn upon our dark understanding, when it became clear that the coincidence in name was due to a common Egyptian origin. This was a large morsel to swallow, not one bite merely, but two; that on one hand Egyptian mariners had crossed the Atlantic, and that some other band or bands of Egyptian explorers had settled in the very heart of Southern England. As we have said, this was a large draught upon our power of believing, but confirmations began to accrue from one quarter and another. Other villages with Egyptian names turned up in the vicinity of Heytesbury. such, for instance, as Sutton Veny which seemed to contain the name of Osiris, and there were Long Barrows not Far ofF which might possibly be claimed as tokens of Egyptian sepulture. Not very far away is the ancient road running East and West which goes by the name of The Harroway. This is certainly one of the oldest roads in the kingdom and shows how persistent the early titles of roads and settlements can be. Here we have conserved for us Heru, the Egyptian name for Horus, just as we have it in Harrow-on-the-Hill or Harrogate in Yorkshire, which is the equivalent of *Heru Khart* or 'Horus the Child'. So we come near to locating in one settlement and its vicinity the four great Samaritan-Egyptian deities which were discovered in Ahab's ivory palace.

It is clear, then, that lsis and Nephthys represent Egypt on Salisbury Plain, and we are entitled to make a similar inference for lsis and Nephthys in the West lndies. If, however, we do this, we have committed Egyptian colonists to the transit of the micfll-Atlantic ages before Columbus; we ought to have seen this at first.

It was during a sojourn on the Hampshire coast that my attention was drawn to the name Great Chalfield, on a neighbouring house. It was evidently a mere importation where it stood, but whence was it derived? The answer was that in Wiltshire, about two and a half miles north-east of Bradford-on-Avon, are the manors of Great Chalfield and Little Chalfield.

But what do these names mean? We have already noted above that Tcher (or Tchar) is one of the names of the great pair of goddesses. It stands for them collectively. It can also be used in a detached form in which the Great Char stands for lsis, and the Little Char for her sister. Could these names be derived from char+field, the customary change from r to l having been observed? If so, the adjectives Great and Little would be in order as an integral part of each name, lsis being the Great Char, and Nephthys the Little Char.

THE CHURCH, GREAT CHALFIELD.

GREAT CHALFIELD MANOR HOUSE.

6

THE MILL, LITTLE CHALFIELD.

A glance at the map gave the following information. Great Chalfield with its manor house and church, and Little Chalfield with a manor house and old water-mill are distant from each other less than half a mile. The former is about a mile north of the village of Holt. An old lane leading from Holt through Chalfield Hatch in the direction of Great Chalfield is called Gipsy Lane, and between the Hatch and the manor house is Lady's Coppice.

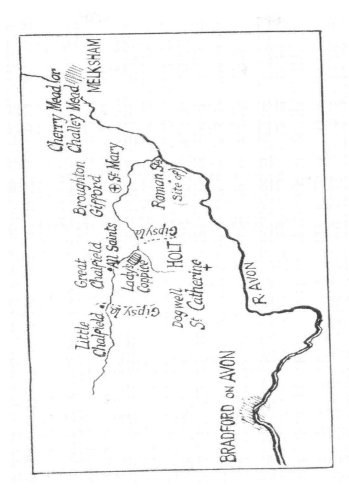

Another Gipsy Lane, now disused, led down to the brook at Little Chalfield from the north. Less than a mile to the east of Great Chalfield is Broughton Gifford.

A visit to Great Chalfield was suggested, though it was difficult to imagine how it could help our enquiry. Was the 'Lady' of Lady's (or is it Ladies?) Coppice Isis or Nephthys?

Did the word Gypsy refer not to Romanys, as it generally does but to people of Egypt? There could hardly be anything here apart from place-names to suggest the former presence of Egyptian sanctities.

Nothing could seem more typically English than the beautiful fifteenth century manor house with its moat and its clipped yew trees, even though the building has a curious architectural feature said to be paralleled only in Cairo. The church stands also within the moat that surrounds the house and is the natural place to look for the conservation of tradition. The dedication is to All Saints and was formerly to St. Catherine, and on the interior walls are the remains of some remarkably fine frescoes dating' from the end of the fifteenth century[3]. These frescoes are not unrelated but constitute a complete series.

They show, first, St. Catherine standing before the Emperor and disputing with him; next, St. Catherine disputing with the pagan philosophers in the presence of the Emperor; thirdly, the scourging of the Saint; fourthly, St. Catherine in prison being visited by the Empress and the Captain of the Guard who kneel before her; fifthly, the miraculous destruction of the spiked wheels by two angels; and lastly, the decapitation of the Saint in the presence of the Emperor. This is the story of St. Catherine of Alexandria. We may say, without fear of contradiction, that Catherine is the greatest of the women saints of the old Egyptian church. Nor would it be a very rash hypothesis to maintain that as such she must have displaced a number of cult centres of Isis, both in Egypt and elsewhere.

We may see that St. Catherine has proprietary rights in this locality in another way. In the village of Holt we observe that the dedication of the church is to St. Catherine. Evidently the Saint was deeply revered in this small area. Reverting to Lady's Coppice, we

---

3   See *The Times* for April 12th, 1938. It was the Tropenell Chapel,
built in the fifteenth century, which was formerly dedicated to
St. Catherine.—E. F. W.]

may remark that the name Holt itself means 'wood' or 'coppice', and that then 'Lady' of Holt is likely to be St. Catherine rather than St. Mary.

Before proceeding to a wider examination of the element *char-* (*tcher-*) in place-names, we will look a little further for possible traces of lsis and Nephthys or other Egyptian deities in this part of Wiltshire.

At Broughton Gifford our attention is drawn in two directions. First of all, it is commonly said that Gifford is a family name that was not associated with Broughton until the late Middle Ages. lt may be so; but we remember that we have in Devonshire, Aveton Gifford and Compton Gifford as well as the closely related Efford - all of which can be traced to an Egyptian ancestry. So we reserve our judgment with regard to this name. More striking are the carvings which came to light when the ivy was removed from over the porch of Broughton Gifford church.

In a niche on either side are two female figures with wings. The figure to the right is slightly larger and has a headdress of some kind. The corresponding ornament on the head of the other has been broken off together with the top of one wing. Each of the angels holds a shield, but there is no coat of arms or other decoration upon it. ls it possible that here a tradition remained of reverence to two female saints? The suggestion is made perhaps less acceptable by the presence at the Saxon church of Bradford-on-Avon of two reclining angels in niches above the chancel. It would be interesting to know how far this is usual. In Bradford-on-Avon, St. Catherine is known as the patroness of the ancient almshouses.

The distance between the river Avon at Bradford and the manor of Great Chalfield is, as we have said, only about two and a half miles, and it is only half that distance from the manor house to the river through Holt.

Now this is a very important observation. It answers for us the question that in one form or another besets the explorer who asks how Egyptian settlements could be found in an in-land county like Wiltshire. The answer is that the colonists reached Wiltshire by water. They came inland from Bristol. The new settlement of the Charfields[4] is not so very far on the old road from Stonehenge itself, just over twenty miles away, It will be remembered that when we were discussing how to get the blue stones of Stonehenge from Pembrokeshire to Wiltshire, we hesitated between a transit by the Bristol Avon or the longer detour by the Christchurch Avon. Such new evidence as we have been collecting appears to be on the side of the Bristol Avon.

When we make the statement that it was possible to go up the Bristol Avon and there find near Bradford a district which might properly be called Egyptian, we are not indulging in conjectures. We have actually found the Egyptian settlement. The pair of sites to which we have been referring are connected by a common philological origin and by a community of religious ideas. The ground form in etymology is the Egyptian word *tcher*, which represents some kind of bird of prey, probably a hawk, and in religion the underlying connection lies in the fact to which we have referred above that *tcher* stands for both lsis and Nephthys. It is both or either. There is, so to speak, a religious subway between the two

---

4 Chalfield is pronounced locally very like *Char*field

manors, or, it we like to say so, they are not really two except by an artificial differentiation. Great and Little in this instance are a connection rather than a distinction.

ANUBIS AGAIN

Before we leave this district we may say that our attention has been drawn by one who is himself a native of the village of Holt to the existence of a 'dog' well there. There are fields on the west side of the village called 'Great Dogwells' and 'Little Dogwells'. The well is now covered in, but its water is reputed to have been valued for its coldness. In our essay on 'The Dog' (Afterglow Essays, No. 3.) we pointed out the occurrence of a 'dogwell' actually named Epwell and showed that it was connected with the cult of Anubis. Near Monkton Farm, in Broughton Gifford, there is a field called Amblecroft. Now Amble is so near in form to Ambo or Anpu (Anubis) that we may confidently say it stands for "dog." Compare the name, for instance, with the hamlet names of Chapel Amble and Lower Amble in the parish of St. Kew in North Cornwall, an area that was once Egyptian. It may also throw' light on the name Gifford in Broughton Gifford.

There is in existence close to Monkton Farm an ancient paved ford across the River, which makes it probable that the name Gifford, or Gip-ford, is here derived from an actual ford rather than from a family name and the proximity of Amble to this ford strengthens the argument.

These names stand for Anubis as we have shown in the essay on 'The Dog'.

We have therefore some evidence for considering the possibility that Broughton Gifford may disclose to us the name of Anubis.

Thus the evidence for an Egyptian settlement in this corner of Wiltshire is cumulative, for we have now two churches with Egyptian dedications - three, if we include Broughton Gifford with its female angelic figures over the porch - a Lady's Wood, and a Gypsy Lane, and only a little way away a 'dog' well and a 'dog' field; while our map shows many more names compounded with *tcher* (Cher- or Char-) such as Cherry (Challey) Mead in Broughton Gifford[5], Charwell Field or Camp near the great earthwork of South Cadbury, Somerset, Cherhill on the way to Avebury, Charbury Hill by Bishopstone and Cherbury Camp, Berkshire, so that we need not doubt that there was an actual Egyptian settlement here.

In determining the philological unity of our two village names we struck into the ground form *tcher,* a pure Egyptian root whose occurrence cannot be limited to a single spot on the borders of Wiltshire. We must ask the question: are there any other *tcher* (Cher-) sites elsewhere to be recognised as Egyptian localities?

Now let us turn to the other migration which certainly took place from the great harbour of Cherbourg in France, to the coast of Dorset. We have previously noted that this name *tcher* was involved in the name of the harbour of Cherbourg, and had been transferred thence to Charmouth in Dorset by Egyptian migrants who had carried it all the way through a group of settlements, Charbury, Cherbury and the like till they reached the Thames at the point where the modern Cherwell stream (pronounced Charwell) flows into the Thames.

In tracing such a line as being involved in the history of Britain and the movements of its first settlers, we had no reason for referring to Egypt at all. Egypt may be there but does not assert itself. The case is, however, quite changed when we introduce the etymological consideration and ask the meaning of *cher* in Cherbourg and of *char* in Dorset, for it is clear that these names are derived directly from an Egyptian ground-form which we have learnt to write as *tcher*. It will follow that when we trace lines of migration from Charmouth inland we are actually identifying Egyptian settlements all the way from Charmouth in Dorset to Cherwell or Charwell on the Thames. We have only to make a little map in aid of our geographical vision to cause us surprise at the extent to which *char-* and *cher-* names are scattered over the area to which we refer. The only difficulty that arises is in the case of such names as exhibit an intrusive letter l, for example, Charlbury with Charbury, etc.

---

5   See Mudge's l-inch Map of Somerset, 1817

It remains to he decided Whether these are true variants or simple diminutives, like St. Austell which is derived from Aust.

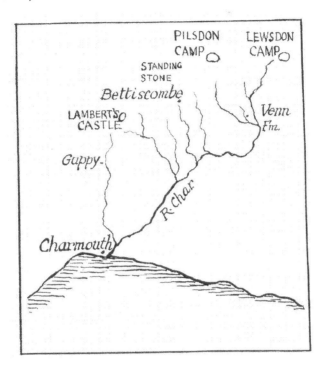

Setting on one side the cases referred to and coming to the Thames itself, we ask whether we can find out anything further about the Cherwell stream. Let us follow the stream away from the Thames from Oxford to King's Sutton and again from King's Sutton to Banbury. We shall be surprised tofind that in following the stream we are moving through an area which is definitely marked with tokens of Egyptian settlement. These will occur on either side of the stream, and even the bridges that cross it have Egyptian elements in their names. For instance here is Doddington, which contains the name of the Tet or Ded pillar of Osiris; and we notice several names beginning with Ast, which will here stand for Isis, whose common name is Ast or Aust[6]. Bodicote implies barley cultivation, and names containing Row, as Rowdon, and Row Barrow, will refer to Ra the Sun God. South of Kings Sutton is Nell (earlier, Neiel) Bridge with two adjacent farms of the same name, and if we follow up the course of the Swere stream we reach Nill Farm, which is really the same name as Nell, while just east of it is FernhiII—we shall

find a Fernhill Farm up a stream to the north-east of Banbury - a name by which we have learnt to recognise a great number of places all over the countryside where there has been a peaceful penetration by Celtic speaking people of settlements which were primarily Egyptian. Fernhill is, as we have shown, a modified form of Fir Nil where Fir is the Celtic for 'men of'. We have brought Egypt to the very verge of the Midlands.

An interesting example of *tchar* sites will be found in the county of Gloucester, where we can find Charfield, and likewise in Somerset, near Bridgwater, we have Charlinch and Little Charlinch. Charfield is interesting not only because of its earlier spelling, but because if we may judge from its position near Wotton-under-Edge, it would appear to have been reached from the Severn rather than the Avon.

In any case, wherever we can detect the ground form *tchar* or *tcher* in the names of places, we may safely infer that we have discovered a primitive Egyptian settlement.

MIGRANT TRAILS

The trail of a migrant or colonising people can often be followed with great closeness, especially where names are wholly or in part repeated. Suppose, for instance, we make a little map of the district around Charborough House and Park. This estate Iies about six miles west of Wimborne in Dorset, and the close agreement of the name, both in sound and in sense, with the harbour of Cherbourg in

---

6   Aust occurs as a personal name in the Parish Registers for Broughton in I715; see Rev. J. Wilkinson, T*he History of Broughton Gifford* (1860)

northern France makes it certain that it was a colony from the latter place which had settled itself in the former. A trail, or trails, from the one will take you to the other, and the prefixed syllable *char-* or *cher-* shows that they were Egyptian settlers addicted to the cult of Isis and Nephthys. A few of these names are seen in the vicinity. This colony probably came by way of Poole Harbour.

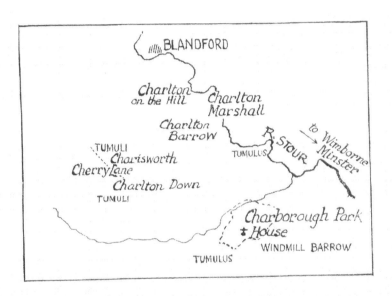

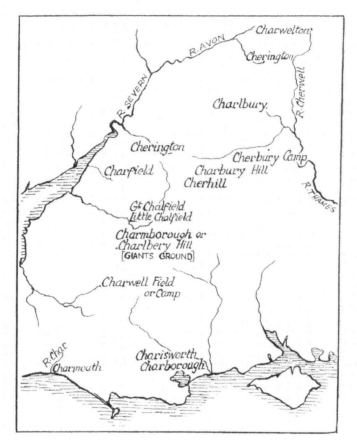

It remains to he decided Whether these are true variants or simple diminutives, like St. Austell which is derived from Aust.

ST. CATHERINE AT BRISTOL AND BATH.

[by E.F. Wills]

The finding of three sites connected with St. Catherine of Alexandria in the district around Bradford-on-Avon, as shown in the foregoing essay, prompts the question as to whether the Saint has left any traces of herself lower down this river, and, also, whether any reasons can be found for supposing that she may have taken the place here too of an earlier Egyptian goddess, or goddesses, venerated by the early settlers when they travelled up the Avon past the sites of Bristol and Bath.

The answer is, that during the fourteenth and fifteenth century, this Saint was accorded very high honour in both Bristol and Bath, and in Bath, at least, there are good reasons for thinking that she superseded an earlier pair of Egyptian goddesses, as will be shown.

It is unnecessary here to give all the historical details relating to St. Catherine in the two cities. We shall just select certain points which may bear upon our problem. In the Bristol area we find St. Catherine's name in connection with three buildings; first the ancient hospital at Bedminster, whose position is marked by the present street name of 'Catherine Mead'. Then there were chapels to her honour in St. Peter's Church, and Temple Church, Bristol.

The Hospital of St. Catherine is thought to have been founded in the thirteenth century. We are told that it lay on a great road of pilgrims, and it was built for their benefit. Like that at St. Cross at Winchester (where, incidentally, there was an altar of St. Catherine in the Chapel) the hospital used to distribute doles to pilgrims, who would doubtless notice the coloured Catherine wheel of cloth sewed to the left breast of the black mantles of the secular priests. The pilgrims would be going, for instance, to Glastonbury in the south, and northwards to the shrine of St. Mary Bellhouse, in St, Peter's, Bristol[7]. Glaston was certainly a centre of pilgrimage in very early

---

7 See *Bristol: as it was and as it is.* pp. 303, 304

times, and it is interesting to find St. Peter's Church[8]——where there was, and still is, a Chapel of St. Catherine described in the early twelfth century as 'the oldest and chiefest of all the Bristol churches'. The foundation is thought to go back to Saxon times.

But it was at Temple or Holy Cross Church, that our Saint received the greatest distinction; for she was patroness of the Guild of Weavers, 'most influential of the old trade fraternities'. It would be interesting to know how the weavers came to be attracted to St. Catherine. Had they learnt their art from Egypt? The patroness of weaving in Greece was Athena herself, and she has been compared with the Egyptian goddess Neith (Net). Perhaps the answer may lie with the Knights Templar. They had an encampment in Bedminster in the twelfth century—the foundations of their oval church have been discovered under the present building—and their church at Temple in Cornwall was dedicated to St. Catherine. These Crusaders are said to have held the tradition that 'there is no other religion than the religion of nature, preserved in the Temples of Initiation in Egypt and Greece.' So far neither the names of Isis or Neith have been found in the old city, but I pointed out in my essay Egypt in Bristol, that the name Venny Lane, a former name of All Saints' Lane, appeared to stand for that of Osiris in titular form, and this hill-side location above the Avon is not far from St. Peter's Church. The name Venny has many parallels in the south-west; compare especially Sutton Veny, near Heytesbury, mentioned above by Dr. Rendel Harris. This find was certainly surprising, and, if correct, it implied some kind of Egyptian influence on the site of the old city. Recently, evidence has been adduced in connection with Sun worship in Bristol, and an interesting inference drawn from its undoubted prominence anciently in this seaport of the West[9].

At Bath, St. Catherine was again a notable figure, but here we shall be able to learn something further about her earlier surroundings. We find her name mentioned as one of the patrons of

---

8   Pryce, *History of Bristol*, gives the dedication as SS. Peter and Paul.
9   H. T. Sherlock, *The Rising Sun*, pp, 12; 46-47.

the Sanctuary Chapel, founded in 1170[10]. In the fifteenth century, the citizen had to take an oath at his admission to the freedom of the city, when he engaged to keep St. Catherine's day as a holy day yearly, and to help to maintain St. Catherine's Chapel and the Bridge. Peach even calls the Saint 'patroness' of the city of Bath; but there is something more to be told. St. Catherine's Chapel was attached to the ancient Hospital of St. Catherine at Bath, and both Collinson and Peach relate the traditional founding of this institution. Here is Collinson's account (History of Somerset, l., p. 44):—

> In a narrow passage, denominated Binbury Lane, near the south-west angle of the Borough walls, are the Bimberries, Black Alms, or Hospital of St. Catherine, founded in ancient times by two sisters of the name of Bimbury. This hospital... was rebuilt by the Corporation of the city in the year 1553. *There was anciently a chapel belonging to this hospital, on the front of which were placed the statues of the co-founders,* but these have long since perished with the chapel itself. [Italics ours]

Peach's version (*Rambles About Bath*, p. 61)) runs thus:—

> St. Catherine's Hospital is stated to have been built by *seven sisters*, of the name of *Binbury* on some arable land within the town wall called [in 1553] '*Bynburye landes*', anciently belonging to a family of that name.
>
> [Italics ours.]

Now we notice that Collinson says there were *two* sisters, and that he adds that their statues were actually placed on the front of the chapel, a statement which looks like good history. If we hesitate to accept Peach's version of *seven* sisters it is not because there is any real impossibility in finding a family of seven sisters all intent on the good work of founding a hospital. It is because the number seven, as

---

10   Peach, *Rambles About Bath*, (1876) p. 40.

is widely recognised, is an ancient religious symbol, of astral significance, and it is found over a wide area - even in India - applied to many natural objects, such as wells, or trees, in cases where the actual number of the particular objects may be only one or two. But its occurrence in this story of the pious sisters is important, for it carries back the tradition a very long way - in fact to pre-Christian times. Again, we note the slight difference in the spelling of the name, *Bin*bury or *Bim*bury, and there is even more confusion to be seen in Peach's *Street Lore of Bath* (1893) where on page 1 he has '*Bymn*bury Lane, a very ancient street', while on page 132 he writes it '*Bin*burie or *Bym*berry Lane'. As we have decided there are *two* sisters, we write their name *Bin*bury[11]. The exact force of the Saxon suffix 'bury' or 'berry', is not quite certain but the whole name might mean 'town (or village) of the two [sisters]'.

On the front of St. Catherine's Chapel 'were placed the statues of the co-founders.' We seem to remember having met with something like this elsewhere—in fact on the porch of St. Mary's Church, Broughton Gifford, only eight miles from Bath, and in a district where St. Catherine was honoured, as the essay has shown. Did the Bath statues possess wings, we wonder? This we shall never know for they have long since perished with the chapel. It is quite possible that they did, for it is evident that our pair of sisters are not merely ladies; they are goddesses - the Egyptian pair, Isis and Nephthys, called *Tchar* or *Tcher.*

If this conclusion is correct we might expect to find traces of the name *Tchar* in the vicinity of Bath. At a distance of under two miles to the north of the Abbey Church of St. Peter and St. Paul, is the ancient parish church of St. Mary at Charlcombe, with a holy well of St. Mary in the adjacent Rectory garden.

With Charlcombe we might possibly bracket a place called Cherlemede near 'la Brodecroft' mentioned in the time of Henry III with other names near Bath.[12] Collinson wrote that the whole village of Charlcombe belonged some time before the Conquest to the Abbey of Bath, and that there was a common tradition that *its church*

---

11   Note again the traces of the dual
12   Somerset Record Society, vol. 7.

was the mother church to Bath. But a visit to the combe and village produced a two-fold connection. Not only was the tradition of the mother church found to be still widely held, but also there was a well-known tradition of *an underground passage* which connected the church with the Abbey, though evidence for its material existence was lacking. There are said to be other such 'tunnels' not many miles away, connecting sacred sites; and, indeed, many examples have been noted in various parts of the country, chiefly in connection with springs and rivers. An Egyptian origin for this widespread belief in a supposed underground passage has been claimed. [13] The proximity of the holy well to the church makes one suspect that it may have been the well at Charlcombe and the springs near the Abbey, or possibly the river Avon, which were originally thought to have been joined by a passage. The name Charlcombe ('Cerlecume' in *Domesday*) then may be explained as due to the ground-form *tchar* or *tcher*, with an intrusive letter l, probably to aid speech. It is St. Mary, however, and not St. Catherine, who has here displaced the *Tchar* goddess at the holy well and church.[14]

On Lansdown and neighbouring downs many barrows and other remains have been noted, thus proving occupation of these heights in prehistoric times.

The Parish of St. Catherine, with its church and adjacent holy well, is some four miles north-east of Bath. The church is said to have been built by the monks of Bath, who possessed the manor from very early times. It lies in the deeply wooded valley of the St. Catherine's Brook, which rises on high ground south of Marshfield (see Map). Close to this spring we shall find a lane marked Gipsy Lane - whatever this may mean here - on the 6-inch Map. There are said to be remains of megaliths in the neighbourhood. The name of Charmey Down (earlier, 'Chermerdune') to the west of this stream again suggests a connection with the Egyptian word *tchar* or *tcher*,

13   Rendel Harris, *Sunset Essays*, No. 2.
14   Collinson states there was anciently a chantry of St. Catherine in Bath Abbey.

though the second syllable requires explanation, and this may not be quite simple. For comparison there is a similar name, *Charm*borough Hill, in Kilmersdon, north Somerset; and earlier forms, '*Charm*bery or *Charl*bery'[15] suggest that an intrusive letter follows the ground-form Char. This latter site is interesting, for here in a field called 'Giants Ground', a chambered barrow was opened in 1909. In the valley below Charmy Down to the west is the ancient manor of Tadwick or Tatwick. This name probably refers to the *Tet* or *Ded* pillar of Osiris, sometimes spelt *Tat*, and it we look again at the photograph from Samaria on the frontispiece of the essay, we see the two *Tcher* goddesses adoring the pillar, so that the names Charmy and Tatwick may be connected in idea.

The 6-inch Map marks a 'Cherry Well', and near it a 'Cherrywell Wood', the former being on the edge of Charmy Down and above the 600 loot level. This well is now piped, and there seems to be no evidence that it was regarded in Christian times as a holy well. We recall the 'Cherry Mead' or 'Challey Mead' in Broughton Gifford. A natural explanation of the name as due to the presence of the tree, in this case the wild cherry, appears to be open to question. For instance, in Devon, there is a 'Cherry Brook' and a 'Cherricornbe', but these names are admittedly of uncertain origin and meaning. In Dorset, alongside of *Charis*worth Farm, on *Charl*ton Down, there is a lane, locally called 'Cherry Lane' (see the Map of Charborough Park and district). It is on high ground and commands wide views, and there are tumuli and other signs of ancient settlement at hand, but upon enquiry locally, the meaning of this name was unknown. Can the element *tcher* be involved? Perhaps further research will throw light on this question.

E. F. WILLS.

---

15   Lord Hylton, *The History of Kilmersdon,* (Index).

NOTE.

We have not space to discuss the by-form of the Egyptian *tcher* ending in a dental sound, e.g., *tchert*. It may be of interest. however, to note the existence of this form, as it may he responsible for the intrusion of a *d* in the late mediaeval spellings of Chalfield. There is no need to resort to the explanation of Chalfield as a 'cold field' in order to account for these.— **R. H.**

SULIS RISING

By Paul Dunne.

The ancient British Goddess Sulis is another example of a once Great Goddess whose records on the inner planes have seemingly again been purposely expunged making it difficult to read the records or form a strong Sulis Contact. Yet a vestigial awareness of Sulis remains strongly and powerfully alive within the racial mind thus indicating that at some point in the history of these islands Sulis was once a well-known Goddess of awesome, and perhaps feared, reputation.

Just a dwelling thought upon Sulis is enough to engender a sense of warm, watery awe and power. With a sense that we in fact ought to know this Goddess and her aspects all too well. Suggesting that her myth, legend, symbolism and guise remains hidden in plain sight within British life and culture to this very day.

Firstly then, what do we actually know about the Goddess Sulis. We know that Sulis was the form of the Great Goddess associated with the Temple Baths, Aqua Sulis, that would eventually give their name to what today is the Somerset city of Bath. These Roman Baths and their naturally heated springs seemingly gave their name to the city. Indeed, to this very day we could say that there is a Shrine to Sulis in every home, albeit it in the form of a bath tub or a power shower. In her most mundane aspect Sulis is the Goddess of the bath or bathing room, as well as all spas, wells and the water mains piping of every village, town and city.

Today the vast network of water piping connects the bathrooms of every home. An aspect of Sulis is thus watery connections, bathing and cleanliness. To bathe or shower is an aspect of true civilisation. Bringing cleanliness, refreshment and helping to keep us free from unpleasant odours and disease. Sulis is thus also a Goddess of Purity, with bathing before robing also being important in some forms of Ritual and Ceremonial Magic we could also say that Sulis represents personal cleansing in a magical sense.

The mysterious origins of Bath have other little known possible links with the mysteries of antiquity that may potentially span back to those of Babylon, Ancient Egypt and Ancient Greece. The link I propose is tenuous, but it contains a strong sense of truth, as the reader may deduce for themselves. The link pertains to the legendary magical figure of Abaris.

Abaris, is known as the High Priest, or Master, of The Hyperborean Mysteries. It is said that the Hyperborean Mysteries have a secret home which is based in North West Europe. This secret home is in fact The British Isles.

Abaris was the servant of the Hyperborean Apollo (Sun God). Abaris is also said to have been an Adept of The Pythagorean Mysteries which within themselves contain a fusion of the Babalonian, Ancient Egyptian and Ancient Greek Mysteries and Magical Systems.

The strange mythos and mysterious linage of Abaris mirrors that of Bladdud, the legendary founder of the pre-Roman city of Bath. It is also said that not only did Bladdud have the ability to fly, but he also started the Temple and Worship of the Goddess Sulis at Bath. Later under Roman occupation Sulis would be renamed Sulis Minerva.

Abaris and Bladdud link the Celtic Mysteries with those of the very earliest ages of The Hermetic Tradition. It is said that the Hyperborean Mysteries, of which Abaris is The Master, are far safer to work with than those of The Atlantean Mysteries.

Bath itself represents The Magical Western Gate in the Lodge Temple of The British Mysteries, and the Magical Energies of 'The Generative Powers of Great Britain'. These Generative Powers and Forces of Great Britain, or Old Albion, are brought to a head within the hot wellsprings of the Temple of Aqua Sulis, or Sulis Minerva, and the through the basin or bowl of the wider city enclave of Bath and this has magical ramifications on the sacred landscape and magical sites surrounding all four contours, or sides of the city of Bath itself. Bath and its surrounding areas are sites linked to Generative Forces.

There is some debate as to the origin and meaning of the word 'Sulis'. It has connotations which suggest that it means 'Eye', 'Eye-Gap', 'Vision', and 'Well'. In addition, the proto-Celtic word 'Suli' would seem to mean 'Sun'. So we might consider Sulis to mean The Solar Eye of The Wells of Vision and thus Far-Seeing and Prophecy. Making Sulis and Oracular Sun Goddess. Akin to a Feminine form of the Masculine Egyptian God Horus, who is now considered to be the God of the current New Age of Aquarius and the New Aeon of Air. Thus it is perhaps now the time of Sulis Rising within the New Age of Aquarius. This also makes me think of the mysterious word 'Aquarius' itself, which with a little word play could be alluding to Aqua-Sirius within the current New Age of Aquarius.

The naturally hot spring water of the Temple of Aqua Sulis has been rising at an apparently pretty exact temperature of 46c for thousands of years. 1,170,000 litres, or 240,000 gallons of water rises up there each day. This natural phenomena was believed by the ancients to be part of the Magical Powers of the Gods. The hot water itself must have seemed reminiscent or akin to the warm amniotic fluids of the womb of the mother in which her baby swims.

The hot spring waters were, like the Goddess Sulis Minerva, considered to have healing and restorative powers. The mineral rich water of this sacred spa spring supplied the magnificent Roman Bath-House which had visitors from across the vast Roman Empire. Sacred offerings were also thrown into the spring there which included more than 12,000 Roman coins, the largest sacrificial haul of coinage ever found within Great Britain. Also found there were metal pans known as 'Paterae' inscribed with the letters 'DSM', or the phrase 'Deae Sulis Minerva'. Meaning 'Goddess Sulis Minerva'. More darkly, there were also a number of messages on lead or pewter that were rolled up and contained curses upon enemies, making Sulis

Minerva also to seem to be a Goddess for Curses and Destruction upon ones enemies.

The senior Western Mystery Tradition writer, Alan Richardson, asked me for my impressions of the following bas relief, or, temple pediment upon the front arch of the Aqua Sulis Temple:

I intuitively recognised this image to be that of the Oldest of the Sea Gods, Pontus. As the oldest and most ancient pre-Olympian Sea God, he was a one of the Greek Primordial Gods. He was 'born without father' the Son of the Un-Manifest Aether and the Earth Goddess Gaia (the Earth Soul or Planetary Being now in the process of becoming The Planetary Spirit). Making Sulis herself the Granddaughter of Gaia, and the Daughter of Pontus. The significance of Sulis only to become fully realised within the current age. Sulis is the most important Goddess of current times as she contains the essence and lessons relevant to our present times and planetary predicament as a species.

(To be Continued...)

APPENDIX 3

The un-Holy Grail

The quest for the Holy Grail has occupied the spiritual life of Western people for centuries now. The attainment of the Grail - whatever it is - has been seen as the ultimate achievement within our experience. The Grail leads us into those purer realms from which there is no need of return. Attain the Grail and the material world is left behind forever.

Now there is perhaps more Grail-related literature on the bookshelves today than for any other spiritual impulse, and more academic light being directed toward the whole Arthurian cultus than any other topic within the Western Tradition. Countless theories expound upon the true nature of the Grail and the 'Grail experience' - all of which must enable us to get a little closer to the thing itself. But there is still one Grail Secret which has scarcely been touched upon at all. It is a secret that is at once obvious, simple, and - like the Emperor's clothes - once revealed can never be ignored again.

Imagine, then, that we are witnessing the Grail Ceremony as it is retold in those basic versions which lurk aback of the popular consciousness... the small room in the enchanted castle, the two pure, sinless, chaste and perfect knights Galahad and Perceval, the mystic communion with the spear dripping blood into the Grail itself, and outside, peering through the window, the gaunt face of Lancelot - denied the experience through his regal sins.

Everyone knows this story. Everyone thrums to it at some time. But now consider this, and answer honestly:

Which modern person with any warmth, heart and passion could really give a damn about those two boring, virginal little prigs? Who could care about the chaste and sinless heaven that they would seek to enter? And, all those tedious esoteric sophistries apart, who could really care about the Grail itself if such dreariness is what it demands?

Galahad and Perceval are dead fish - the last surges of the Piscean Era drawing into itself - and the Grail is their vessel. Like any other spiritual experience the Grail Vision is something that the Western world should have let flow through, and then on, with appropriate blessings. Instead, we have clung to it. And to cling to any spiritual experience is to create a tyranny for ourselves. In its own luminous, beautiful, and impossibly pure way, the Holy Grail has held the inner life of the West in thrall for a long time now.

But that is not the last/lost secret of the Grail Ceremony. That is to be found, not in Galahad or Perceval or the Grail itself, but through the "face in the window." It is the great du Lac who holds those formulae which will take us into the next Age. An Age when the Grail will retreat to its proper place - although this smacks of occult heresy even to suggest such a thing. But if coming Ages cast their shadows before, then Lancelot is the foreshadowing of that Man Carrying Water who will stride us into Aquarius.

Though be aware that this is not going to happen soon. Forget all the shining eyed New Age, smashey and nicey attitudes. The sun will not arise in the constellation of Aquarius for another 300 years or so. Until then, we're stuck in that damned chalice with those cold fish, and we have to reach beyond the rim.

There is no suggestion here that Lancelot of the Lake ever had any historical basis, although attempts have been made to identify him as an alter ego of Gawaine, the "Hawk of May." Taught by enchantresses in a submarine world, Lancelot rose from the waters by his own impulse - imagery which is extremely important for those who understand. He is very much a creature of the Green Ray, a son of the Celtic Otherworld, and although this seems incongruous, it is a fact that military people are especially good at exploring the depths of this Ray. They have the discipline to get back, which many lack. They understand something of its cruelty, too.

Lancelot may well be a very potent faery being on the inner planes with his/its own uncompromising agenda. But for most of us he can best be seen as strata of consciousness, which can be reached, via the telesmic imagery of his Myth.

Contact with du Lac is unmistakable: a brooding sort of compassion; a grave kind of sympathy; the grizzled heart of a simple man made wise by a lifetime of battles, both within and without. There are hints of darkness, flashes of cruelty, and a capacity for ruthlessness as a last resort.

It is not a contact that can be sustained for long, nor is it an intellectual contact. Intelligent and simple, yes; intellectual and sophisticated, most definitely not. Yet it shows us a Way - narrow and fraught though It is - which can lead us into Wonder. It is the path of the warrior who chooses his Queen, the archetypal Woman, above any other revelation, and who will forsake the Christ-centred Heaven for another sort of reality.

In this wise, a study of that dragon legend of the Laidly Worm, which links with his castle in Northumberland, will repay the effort a thousand times. It was originally named Castle Dolorous; when he fell in love with Guinevere, he renamed it Joyous Gard. You can almost give your heart to him because of his sheer hopefulness. Lancelot may have been the creation of medieval story-tellers, but the magickal impulse behind him is ancient.

Because he can be contacted using a telesmic image, it is quite permissible to make plays upon his name. Thus Lancelot du Lac = Lance à l'eau du Lac, with the simple but tantalising connotations that this holds. And with Lancer meaning "to throw," then Lancer L'eau brings us back to the image of Aquarius pouring out the water from his pitcher. And again there is *Lance* and *lot* meaning luck or chance. The Lance of Destiny? The Spear of Luck? There is an arcanum concealed there too. This is certainly weak translation but the magick behind it is strong.

And we can wonder, too, at his very 'Frenchness'. Britain and France have a tanist relationship. In primordial times there was no sea between them and they shared, of course, the same rock strata. If we could, in some sense, reach that bedrock under the sea of our national consciousness, then we would reach a common level in which things Gallic would seep into our visions and dreams. This does in fact happen when a certain Magickal Current is touched, although it is a topic too complex to go into here. Likewise, when the two nations have recurring ideas about uniting politically, as Churchill suggested in 1940, or via physical means such as bridges or tunnels, then we can be sure that this same Current is being activated and worked right fiercely.

There is nothing cozy or cute about the du Lac contact, then. Nor is it easy to fix, for it seems to oscillate somewhere between those qualities needed to be the Guardian for the Realms of the Queen at one extreme, and the dark heart of the Sacrificial Priest "who knows things" at the other. But make the contact and you will be touching the very pulse of the Aquarian Age, with all the love and terror and marvel it will hold.

APPENDIX 4

Cattern Cakes
from the:
Kingsdown, Lynsted and Norton Newsletter

INGREDIENTS:

- 9 ounces self-raising flour
- 1/4 teaspoon ground cinnamon
- 2 ounces currants
- 2 ounces ground almonds
- 2 teaspoons caraway seeds
- 6 ounces caster sugar
- 4 ounces melted butter
- 1 medium eggs, beaten
- extra sugar, for sprinkling
- extra cinnamon, for sprinkling

METHOD:

Pre-heat oven to 200C/400F/Gas 6.

Sift the flour and cinnamon into a bowl and stir in the currants, almonds, caraway seeds and sugar and the dried yeast if used.

Add the melted butter and beaten egg.

If using fresh yeast, mix with 1oz of the sugar until liquefied and add at this point. Mix well to give a soft dough.

Roll out onto a floured board to give a rectangle about 12"x10". Brush dough with water and sprinkle with the extra sugar and cinnamon.

Roll up like a Swiss roll and cut into ¾" slices.

Place these slices spaced well apart, on a greased tray and bake for 20 minutes. Take care not to overcook as they can become too hard.

Cool on a wire rack. Sprinkle with extra caraway seeds if liked.

(Modern versions of this recipe use self-raising flour and omit the yeast. The old versions with yeast are much more authentic and taste better.)

iENDNOTES

i   *Me, mySelf and Dion Fortune,* Create-Space Publishing, 2015

ii   *Sex and Light,* Twin Eagles Publishing 2010

iii   *The Magdalen Manuscript,* Tom Kenyon and Judy Sion.

iv   *Waters of the Gap,* p 26, R.J. Stewart   Ashgrove Press 1989

v   *Isis and Nephthys in Wiltshire and Elsewhere.* Rendel Harris and E.F. Wills. Wiltshire Archives ATW917.

vi   *The Cygnus Key,* Andrew Collins

vii   *The Canopus Revelation,* Philip Coppens, 2004.

viii   *Lyra,* Issue 32, 'That photo of Dion Fortune? It's probably not her, you know.'

ix   *Holy Wells of Bath & Bristol Region,* p 39. Phil Quinn Logaston Press

x   *Atlantis – the Stonehenge Enigma*   Robert John Langdon

xi   De Havilland Venom; F 18 Hornet; A10 Warthog.

xii   https://insearchofholywellsandhealingsprings.com

xiii   newdawnmagazine.com; http://tinyurl.com/qch9m3o

xiv   *Short Circuits – Essays in Otherness.* Create Space

xv   *Waters of the Gap,* p 79, R.J. Stewart   Ashgrove Press 1989

xvi   http://www.gmkelly.com/swordhor.html

xvii   *Penetration,* Ingo Swann, p73. Swann-Ryder Prodns. 1999

Printed in Great Britain
by Amazon